ANDREW CARNEGIE

ANDREW CARNEGIE

INDUSTRIAL PHILANTHROPIST

LAURA B. EDGE

LERNER PUBLICATIONS COMPANY/MINNEAPOLIS

To Gerry, Jeremy, and Jonathan

Lerner Publications Company
A division of Lerner Publishing Group
241 First Avenue North
Minneapolis, Minnesota 55401 U.S.A.

Website address: www.lernerbooks.com

Library of Congress Cataloging-in-Publication Data

Edge, Laura Bufano, 1953–
    Andrew Carnegie / by Laura B. Edge.
        p.   cm. — (Lerner biographies)
    Includes bibliographical references and index.
    Summary: Chronicles the rags-to-riches tale of a Scottish
immigrant who used most of the millions he earned as a steel
tycoon to set up a fund for the advancement of science, education,
and peace.
    ISBN: 0–8225–4965–4 (lib. bdg. : alk. paper)
    1. Carnegie, Andrew, 1835–1919. 2. Industrialists—United
States—Biography. 3. Philanthropists—United States—Biography.
[1. Carnegie, Andrew, 1835–1919. 2. Industrialists. 3. Philanthropists.]
I. Title.
CT275.C3 E34 2004
936.2'19—dc21   2002152936

Manufactured in the United States of America
1 2 3 4 5 6 – JR – 09 08 07 06 05 04

CONTENTS

As promised, Andrew Carnegie, left front of carriage, *returned with his mother,* center front of carriage, *to his hometown of Dunfermline, Scotland, a wealthy man.*

ONE

Triumphant Return

1881

On July 27, 1881, at four o'clock in the afternoon, forty-five-year-old Andrew Carnegie sat beside his mother, Margaret, on the front bench of a splendid coach drawn by four sleek horses. The coach rolled into his hometown of Dunfermline, Scotland, under a banner reading, Welcome Carnegie, Generous Son. The national flags of Scotland, England, and the United States fluttered from the gate tower of Dunfermline's old Stewart Palace.

Carnegie's return to Dunfermline fulfilled a promise he had made to his mother. At age twelve, Andrew and his family had moved from Scotland to the slums of Allegheny, Pennsylvania. Life proved hard for the family, and one day Andrew had found his mother weeping. He told her not to cry, promising that one day they would be rich and ride in a fine coach. His mother replied, "That will do no good over here, if no one in Dunfermline can see us." Andrew vowed that he would take his mother to Dunfermline in a handsome coach-and-four (a carriage pulled by four horses), and the whole town would see them.

Thirty-three years had passed since that dark day in Pennsylvania. By then, Andrew Carnegie had built the largest steel company in the United States, Carnegie Brothers & Company. He had become wealthy beyond his wildest dreams and could at last fulfill his childhood promise to his mother.

The ancient town of Dunfermline sits nestled among gently rolling hills and glens in eastern Scotland. Beyond the hills lie the sparkling blue waters of the Firth of Forth. On the day Carnegie and his mother arrived in Dunfermline, with a group of close friends, even the weather cooperated to make it a joyous occasion. According to Carnegie, "The sun shone forth as if glad to shine upon this most memorable day of my mother's life or of mine."

Men, women, and children, dressed in their Sunday best, lined the town's streets. Amid shouts and cheers from the crowd of twenty thousand, the glossy black and red coach entered Carnegie's favorite spot on earth. In a herringbone suit and white top hat, Carnegie stood holding the reigns of the coach. Margaret, clad in a plain black dress and black bonnet, sat beside her son.

A huge parade, eight thousand strong, complete with brass bands and Scottish bagpipes, marched through the streets. The parade turned onto Moodie Street and stopped in front of the stone cottage where Carnegie had been born. At the tolling of the Dunfermline Abbey bells, memories of his childhood washed over Carnegie. Tears flowed freely down his cheeks.

Seventy-one-year-old Margaret Carnegie laid the cornerstone of a public library that her son had donated to his hometown. Carnegie hoped the children of Dunfermline would use the library to discover, as he had discovered, "the most precious of all earthly possessions—books."

Dunfermline Abbey, the burial place of Scottish kings, held a special place in Carnegie's memory.

Carnegie's trip back to Dunfermline illustrated his belief that "in this world we must learn not to lay up our treasures, but to enjoy them day by day as we travel the path we never return to." Andrew Carnegie's life led him down a path filled with stunning business success, intense patriotism, ruthless greed, and genuine humanitarianism. He certainly enjoyed the trip.

Carnegie was born in this two-story Dunfermline house at the corner of Moodie Street and Priory Lane on November 25, 1835.

Two

Simple Beginnings

1835–1848

The sentimental millionaire who swept grandly into Dunfermline, Scotland, began life in modest circumstances. Andrew Carnegie was born on November 25, 1835, in a gray stone cottage on Moodie Street. His father, a weaver, kept his loom in the lower room of the tiny house. A single attic room served as the family's living quarters.

His mother, Margaret Morrison Carnegie, was the most important person in young Andrew's life. According to him, "Anything low, mean, deceitful, shifty, coarse, underhanded, or gossipy was foreign to that heroic soul." William Carnegie, Andrew's father, excelled as a weaver of fine damask linen, an art dating to medieval times. Two-thirds of the population of Dunfermline depended upon that same occupation for their livelihood.

When Andrew was a year old, the family moved to a larger house on Edgar Street. Will Carnegie bought three more looms and hired apprentices, or trainees, to work them. His workshop occupied the lower floor, and the family lived on the second floor.

A Scottish weaver works at his loom. Carnegie's father, Will, worked in similar conditions at his Edgar Street workshop.

The living quarters, reached by an outside stone staircase, were much larger than their previous home.

Amid the clack, clack, clacking of the looms, Andrew would sit for hours watching his father create shimmering images of birds, leaves, flowers, and fruit on fine linen fabric. Like the other weavers in Dunfermline, Will Carnegie prided himself on being a skilled craftsman. He fully expected Andrew to follow the family tradition and become a weaver, too.

Andrew's best friend and constant companion as a child was his cousin George "Dod" Lauder. They called each other "Dod" and "Naig" because, according to Carnegie, "I could not say 'George' in infancy and he could not get more than 'Naig' out of Carnegie."

Dod's father, George Lauder Sr., had a huge impact on the impressionable young boys. He spent hours entertaining them with stories of Scottish history, especially the brave deeds of their hero, Scottish patriot William Wallace. Dunfermline provided a rich backdrop for learning about history. Scotland's King Robert the Bruce was buried in the Dunfermline Abbey. A single crumbling wall remained of a royal palace where Mary, Queen of Scots once held court. Through his stories, George Lauder brought those historical sites to life for Andrew and Dod. As Carnegie would later recall, "No bright child of Dunfermline can escape the influence of the Abbey, Palace, and Glen. These touch him and set fire to the latent spark within, making him something different and beyond what, less happily born, he would have become."

Young Carnegie enjoyed hearing George Lauder's stories about the heroic deeds of Scottish hero William Wallace, right.

George Lauder also introduced Andrew and Dod to the works of Scottish poet Robert Burns and English playwright William Shakespeare. The boys often memorized long passages from these works and recited them wearing paper crowns and wielding paper swords. George Lauder gave the boys a penny for each new play they learned. Andrew saved his pennies in an old sock.

Andrew's first business venture sprang from a pair of rabbits his father brought home one day. Andrew wanted to keep them as pets. His mother pointed out that when baby rabbits appeared, as they did a short time later, there would not be enough food for them. Andrew promised he'd find a way to feed the rabbits without touching the family garden. He kept his promise by hiring neighborhood boys to pick clover and dandelions in the woods as food for the rabbits. As payment, Andrew named a baby rabbit for each of the boys. The plan worked, and the baby rabbits grew plump and healthy.

Andrew attended the Rolland Street School, the least expensive school in Dunfermline. A single large classroom accommodated between 150 and 180 children of all ages. Robert Martin, the schoolmaster, depended heavily on a leather whip to maintain discipline. Andrew didn't feel the sting of that whip, though. He enjoyed school, behaved, and was unhappy if anything prevented his attendance. Shorter than most boys his age, with blue eyes and blond hair, Andrew was labeled "Martin's pet" by his classmates.

In 1843 Andrew became a big brother when his mother gave birth to a baby boy named Thomas. That year, a steam-powered textile factory opened in Dunfermline. The factory's power looms wove fabric faster and more cheaply than Will Carnegie's hand looms. Many of Will's customers began buying their linen from the factory. As his business declined, Will Carnegie sold all but one of his looms and let his apprentices go. The family moved to a smaller cottage not far from Andrew's birthplace. "Shortly after this I began to learn what poverty meant," Andrew recalled.

Andrew's childhood took place during a time of social unrest in Scotland—a time of struggle between rich and poor. In Scotland, England, and other parts of Great Britain, a small group of people, called the nobility, held titles such as lord, duke, earl, and baron. These titles were inherited, or passed down, through the generations. A person who was born into nobility in Great Britain had wealth, land, and political power. Ordinary working people, on the other hand, had very little power. Most of them didn't even have the right to vote.

Andrew spent many hours listening to his father and to his mother's brother, Tom Morrison, discuss the injustices of this system. He cheered as they spoke at political rallies, where they shared their dislike for nobility and discussed ways to improve life for Scotland's working people. Their views angered many wealthy people in Dunfermline. In fact, the owners of the Pittencrieff estate, the most beautiful park in the town, barred Andrew and his relatives from visiting there, because of the family's radical political beliefs.

In the summer of 1847, another steam-powered textile factory opened in Dunfermline. Will Carnegie's business declined even more. Life turned bleak for the family that winter as harsh gusts of wind from the North Sea blasted the tiny village. A tired and discouraged Will announced to his son, "Andra, I can get nae mair work" ("Andrew, I can get no more work").

Andrew's mother stepped in and took charge. She opened a small shop in the front of the house, where she sold flour, salt, cabbages, potatoes, leeks, and "sweeties" to the neighbors. Late into the night, she stitched shoes for her brother, Tom, the leading shoemaker in the village.

The winter of 1847 convinced Margaret Carnegie that the family had to make a change. In 1840, her younger sisters, Annie Aitken and Kitty Hogan, had moved with their husbands to Pittsburgh, Pennsylvania, in the United States. Their letters home to Scotland painted a gloomy picture of American life at first. But by 1847, their husbands had found steady employment, and Annie and Kitty encouraged Margaret to join them. She and Will decided it was time to move. Leaving their home and country was not easy for the Carnegies, but they felt they had no choice.

Margaret sold the family furniture and dishes. Will Carnegie reluctantly sold his one remaining loom. But the family still didn't have enough money to book passage on a ship to America. Margaret's childhood friend Ailie Ferguson Henderson loaned the family her life savings of twenty pounds, enough for the trip.

Uncle Lauder and Dod went to the Edinburgh dock to see the travelers off. Twelve-year-old Andrew couldn't bear to leave them. He ran to his uncle, threw his arms around him, and sobbed. A sailor gently lifted Andrew onto the deck of a waiting boat, a steamer that would take the family to Glasgow, Scotland's biggest city.

In Glasgow the Carnegies boarded an eight-hundred-ton converted whaling ship named the *Wiscasset,* bound for America. The ship was crowded, the food miserable. Most of the passengers spent the fifty-day trip suffering from seasickness. As they lay moaning in their bunks, Andrew reveled in the adventure of the trip. He loved watching the great sails fill with wind, and his cheerful optimism made him a favorite of the sailors. In no time at all, Andrew was helping them with

The Carnegies were among thousands of European immigrants who arrived in America at New York City's Castle Garden, a major port.

their chores and sharing in their Sunday delicacy of plum duff, a cakelike dessert.

On July 15, 1848, the *Wiscasset* docked at Castle Garden in New York City. According to Andrew, "The arrival at New York was bewildering . . . the bustle and excitement of it overwhelmed me." The Carnegies had three more difficult weeks of travel ahead of them to reach their relatives in Pittsburgh. Since railroads did not extend to the city, the travelers took a roundabout voyage by canal boat and steamboat, inching their way along the Hudson River, the Erie Canal, the Mohawk River, Lake Erie, the Ohio Canal, and finally the Ohio River to Pittsburgh.

Margaret Carnegie's sisters welcomed the family warmly. They lived in a neighborhood known as Slabtown, in Allegheny, two miles from Pittsburgh. The Carnegies moved into a flimsy, dark frame house, facing a muddy back alley. From this dilapidated shanty, Andrew Carnegie began to build his fortune.

Smoke from factories often choked the air in Pittsburgh during the industrial revolution of the mid-nineteenth century.

THREE

Climbing the Ladder
1848–1853

Pittsburgh sits at the junction of the Monongahela, Allegheny, and Ohio Rivers in western Pennsylvania. The city's location, perfect for transporting manufactured goods, aided its growth as an industrial center. By the mid-nineteenth century, fast industrial growth also made Pittsburgh one of the dirtiest, ugliest cities in the United States. Narrow unpaved streets, jammed with carriages and wagons, bustled with people hurrying to and from sooty factories. Accustomed to the scenic beauty of Dunfermline, the smoke-filled air of Pittsburgh presented a stark change for twelve-year-old Andrew.

After settling into their new home, the Carnegies searched for work. Will Carnegie rented a small loom and began weaving tablecloths. He sold them door-to-door with meager success. Margaret Carnegie bound shoes for a neighborhood shoemaker. Andrew's little brother, Tom, started school. Andrew set out to find a job.

A man named Blackstock, a fellow Scottish immigrant, owned and operated a cotton mill. He offered Andrew a job.

The position operating a spindle, a device used for winding thread, paid $1.20 a week. Mr. Blackstock also hired Will Carnegie, who left his loom so that he could watch over his son.

After a short time, John Hay, another Scot, offered Andrew a job in his factory for two dollars a week. The factory made bobbins, a kind of spindle. Will Carnegie had had enough of factory work. He drifted back to his loom and once again began weaving tablecloths by hand. He peddled his wares on the streets of Pittsburgh and rode steamboats up and down the Ohio River searching for buyers.

Andrew and his father arrived at the factory before daylight and worked until after dark, six days a week. Will Carnegie loathed the work, but Andrew was pleased to be helping support his family. "I cannot tell you how proud I was when I received my first week's own earnings," he wrote. "One dollar and twenty cents made by myself and given to me because I had been of some use in the world!"

Like these boys, young Carnegie worked in a bobbin factory (rows of bobbins appear at right).

At the factory, Andrew ran a small steam engine and fired a boiler, or water heater, in the cellar. The responsibility weighed heavily on him. He often woke up in the middle of the night, worrying that he'd set the steam gauges too low, causing workers to complain that they didn't have enough power, or that he'd set them too high, causing the boiler to burst.

To his immense relief, Hay needed office help and asked to see a sample of Andrew's penmanship. Pleased with the boy's writing, Hay assigned Andrew the task of preparing his weekly financial statements and writing his correspondence. Andrew liked the job, but since it didn't take much time, he still had to work in the factory. His new responsibilities included dipping newly made bobbins into vats of hot oil. The smell of the oil nauseated him, but Andrew never told his family. At thirteen, he considered himself a man and felt that, "no man would whine and give up—he would die first."

Having tasted the ease of office work, Andrew set out to escape the disgusting vats of oil by making himself more valuable to Hay. He'd heard that all great businesses used the double-entry accounting, or bookkeeping, system. Andrew planned to change Hay's single-entry system to the double-entry system. But first he had to learn accounting. During the winter of 1848–49, Andrew enrolled in a night school class in Pittsburgh. He talked several friends into joining him. After working twelve hours in the factory, the boys trudged across the bridge to Pittsburgh and learned double-entry accounting.

Andrew never converted Hay's accounting system, for in the spring of 1849, he found a better job. During a game of checkers, David Brooks, the manager of a Pittsburgh telegraph office, told Andrew's uncle Thomas Hogan that he was looking for a messenger boy. Andrew tried to convince his father that he was old enough to handle a position that paid $2.50 a week.

Although he was skeptical, Will Carnegie agreed to let Andrew talk to Mr. Brooks.

On a bright sunny day, dressed in his one white linen shirt and Sunday suit, Andrew walked with his father the two miles from Allegheny to Pittsburgh. When they reached the telegraph office, Andrew asked his father to wait outside while he talked to Mr. Brooks. He thought he would make a better impression on his future employer without his old-fashioned father hovering about. Brooks looked Andrew over, asked a few questions, and then asked when he could start work. Andrew said he could start immediately. He became so engrossed in learning his new job that he forgot about his father waiting outside on the street. As soon as it dawned on him, Andrew ran outside and told his father about his new position.

In the mid-nineteenth century, the telegraph allowed high-speed communication between businesses in distant cities. Telegraph messages were sent over electric wires in a writing system called Morse code. When a message came in over the wires, dots and dashes printed on paper. An operator translated the dots and dashes into letters of the alphabet. Once the whole message was translated, the operator handed it to a messenger boy, who darted out and delivered it. The telegraph quickly became an essential tool of newspapers, railroads, the government, and other organizations.

The job as telegraph messenger boy was a turning point in Andrew's life. "From the dark cellar running a steam-engine at two dollars a week, begrimed with coal dirt, without a trace of the elevating influences of life, I was lifted into paradise, yes, heaven, as it seemed to me, with newspapers, pens, pencils, and sunshine about me.... I felt that my foot was upon the ladder and that I was bound to climb."

Young Carnegie took a job as a messenger boy. He wore a cap and uniform similar to those of the messengers above.

To speed up that climb, Andrew set out to become a more efficient messenger boy. He spent hours each night memorizing the names of every business on every street in downtown Pittsburgh. When he had mastered that, he concentrated on learning the faces and names of each person at each business. In his uniform of dark green knickerbockers (knickers), jacket, and cap, Andrew quickly became known around Pittsburgh as "young Andy."

Each telegraph delivered outside the city limits paid the messenger an extra ten cents. Arguments frequently broke out between the boys about who would deliver these valuable "dime messages." To settle the dispute, Andrew proposed pooling the extra money and then dividing the cash equally among the boys at the end of each week. This arrangement worked to everybody's satisfaction and made for a more peaceful workplace.

When telegraphs had to be delivered to the old Pittsburgh Theater, Andrew did his best to snatch them before the other messengers. The manager of the theater allowed messengers to slip up to the gallery to watch William Shakespeare's plays. Andrew soaked up the beauty of the old theater—the rose-colored boxes, crimson seats edged with velvet, gold embroidered draperies, and crystal chandeliers. By listening to the actors, he discovered that skillfully arranged words contained a special kind of magic.

Mr. Brooks required messengers to arrive at work one hour before opening time to sweep and clean the office. Andrew would quickly complete his chores, then spend the rest of the hour teaching himself how to send and receive telegraph messages. Before long, he began filling in for the operators when they took breaks. In 1851 the company promoted

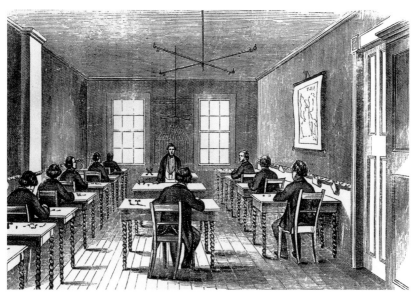

Telegraph operators deciphering code. Carnegie's dedicated study of Morse code quickly earned him a job as an operator.

Andrew to full-time operator, earning what he considered the enormous salary of twenty dollars per month. Between his earnings and those of his parents, the family was able to repay Ailie Ferguson Henderson the money she had loaned them for the trip to America.

Rumors began drifting through the telegraph office that some operators in other cities could take messages by ear— by hearing the dots and dashes rather than reading the printout. Andrew wanted to be the first person in the Pittsburgh office to master the skill. With his characteristic drive and tenacity, he quickly succeeded, becoming only the third operator in the United States to accomplish this feat. Before long, Andrew had the reputation as the best telegraph operator in Pittsburgh. People even came to the telegraph office to watch him work.

Thomas A. Scott, superintendent of the Western Division of the Pennsylvania Railroad Company, noticed Andrew. Scott needed his own telegraph operator and wondered if he could persuade Andrew to work for him. Scott's clerk told him that Andrew would never leave his current position. When Andrew heard this comment, he said, "Not so fast. He can have me."

Andrew shrewdly recognized that the railroad business, which was growing quickly throughout the United States, provided greater opportunities for advancement than the telegraph office. And so, at age seventeen, Andrew began work for the Pennsylvania Railroad at thirty-five dollars per month. He couldn't imagine what he was going to do with so much money!

The Pennsylvania Railroad's depot at Duquesne, Pennsylvania, around 1850. The railroad improved travel for businessmen and other passengers, providing direct and rapid transportation.

FOUR

The Goose That Laid the Golden Egg

1853–1859

When Carnegie joined the Pennsylvania Railroad in 1853, the company had just completed a track between Pittsburgh in western Pennsylvania and Philadelphia in the east. Local businessmen were thrilled, as this meant they no longer had to depend on roundabout trips by water to reach Philadelphia. But because there was just one track, trains going in opposite directions had to share it. When two trains approached each other, one would move to a siding, or sidetrack, to let the other pass. Telegraph operators, such as Carnegie, sent messages to stations along the route to prevent collisions.

Carnegie found sending and receiving telegraphs for the railroad fascinating. He learned the basics of railroading, and, since railroads transported goods between buyers and sellers, he gained a wealth of knowledge about business in general. He studied cargo shipments, tracked market conditions, and learned which businesses succeeded and which failed.

Carnegie worked for Thomas A. Scott at the Pennsylvania Railroad. Scott's strength of character and savvy management skills impressed Carnegie.

His job at the railroad placed Carnegie in daily contact with his boss, Thomas Scott, who quickly became Carnegie's hero. Scott, employed since age ten, had helped care for his mother and ten siblings after his father died. When Carnegie went to work for him, handsome twenty-nine-year-old Scott, with his long, curling side whiskers, cut a dashing figure. He was gentle and charming, yet exuded an aura of power. Carnegie looked up to his boss, considered a genius in railroad management, and learned everything he could from him. Scott also developed a deep affection for Carnegie and became protective of him, calling him "My boy, Andy."

At the railroad, luck was with Carnegie from the start. Shortly after he joined the company, he rode the train from Pittsburgh to Altoona, in central Pennsylvania. He was assigned to pick up the payroll, a package of money for paying the railroad employees in Pittsburgh. On the trip home, Carnegie tucked the package under his vest because it was too large to fit in his pocket. He rode in the front cab of the train, alongside the engineer as the train wound through the Allegheny Mountains and rattled down steep inclines. The jostling of the train shook the package loose. Before long, Carnegie discovered it was missing.

Carnegie knew that losing the payroll might mean the end of his career with the railroad. He begged the engineer to back up the train so he could look for the package. As the train backed slowly down the track, Carnegie spotted the package lying on the bank of a large stream, within a few feet of the water. He jumped off the train and grabbed the money, elated that luck was with him on that bumpy ride from Altoona.

Carnegie once lost a valuable payroll package while riding along this steep, winding railroad line between Altoona and Pittsburgh.

Carnegie's developing leadership skills were tested when he was left to manage a railroad accident in Scott's absence.

Another time, Carnegie reached the office one morning and found that a huge accident had taken place on the railroad. Trains in both directions were at a standstill. Carnegie tried to reach Scott, the only person authorized to give orders to fix the situation, but could not locate him. So Carnegie took matters into his own hands, knowing that he could lose his job if he made a mistake. He plunged in, gave orders in Scott's name, and had everything running smoothly by the time Scott reached the office.

When Scott arrived, Carnegie told him what had happened and showed him the orders he had sent. Scott carefully looked over the reports, then looked at the squirming, nervous Carnegie. Without saying a word, Scott turned and walked to his own desk. He did not mention the incident. Carnegie worried that he might be punished, until he heard from the head of the railroad's freight department that Scott had bragged about what "that little white-haired Scotch devil of mine" had done.

In their free time, Carnegie and his neighborhood friends formed a debating club to discuss the important political issues of the day. Finding enough books to read became a problem for the group, since there were no public libraries in Pittsburgh at the time. "There came, however, like a blessing from above, a means by which the treasures of literature were unfolded to me," Carnegie recalled.

Colonel James Anderson, a retired manufacturer, opened his private collection of more than four hundred volumes to working boys. Each Saturday, Carnegie borrowed a book, reading it throughout the day, whenever he could snatch a few minutes. The following Saturday, he would return it and check out another. Carnegie eagerly devoured all the American history books he could find, as well as essays, biographies, and Shakespeare's plays.

The library became so popular that Colonel Anderson expanded it by several hundred volumes and moved it to its own building. Called the Mechanics' and Apprentices' Library, the new library charged a two-dollar annual fee to most users but was free to all apprentices. The first time Carnegie appeared at the library, the librarian insisted that he pay the fee, since he wasn't an apprentice. Outraged that he should have to pay, Carnegie took the story to the press.

He wrote a letter to the *Pittsburgh Dispatch,* summarizing the history of Colonel Anderson's library and pointing out its many benefits to the boys of Pittsburgh. He also explained that he was a working boy, although not an apprentice, and that he believed Colonel Anderson would want him to have access to the library free of charge.

A short time later, Carnegie received news that Anderson had read the letter and had expanded free library privileges to all working boys under a certain age. The experience convinced Carnegie of the power of the printed word.

Despite his busy schedule, Carnegie always found time to write to his Uncle Lauder and cousin Dod in Dunfermline. In these letters, Carnegie shared his thoughts about his adopted country, which he quickly embraced as his own. In one letter, he contrasted the American and British forms of government: "The one exhibits the vigor of manhood, the other the lassitude of old age, and while the one continues in the old well beaten track the other is continually exploring new paths, presenting new truths and acting on new principles, which a too conservative world cannot but admire though dare not imitate."

Carnegie identified with the young, maturing United States. In many ways, the contrast between his old and new homes mirrored the contrast between his father and himself. While Andrew flourished in America, Will Carnegie could not adapt to the new industrial world. He found fewer and fewer buyers for his wares and finally put aside his loom for good. He spent months in bed with an illness that his physician couldn't diagnose. On October 2, 1855, at fifty-one years old, Will Carnegie died.

In the spring of 1856, Thomas Scott encouraged Carnegie to buy ten shares of stock in the Adams Express Company. Adams Express offered businesses a safe way to transport financial documents and other important materials between big cities such as Boston and New York. The company sent documents by rail and was building thousands of miles of railroad track across the country.

Scott explained that purchasing the stock would give Carnegie partial ownership in the company. If Adams Express

THIS COMPANY HAS FACILITIES UNSURPASSED BY THOSE OF ANY OTHER EXPRESS LINE IN THE WORLD, FOR THE SAFE & EXPEDITIOUS FORWARDING & PROMPT DELIVERY OF

BANK-NOTES, GOLD & SILVER COIN, PARCELS, PACKAGES, FREIGHT, &c

ALSO, FOR THE COLLECTION OF NOTES, DRAFTS & ACCOUNTS, IN ALL THE CITIES, TOWNS & VILLAGES IN THE EASTERN, WESTERN, SOUTHERN & SOUTH-WESTERN STN

With an eye on the future, Carnegie took the advice of his boss, Thomas Scott, and invested in the Adams Express Company. He came to call investment "the goose that lays the golden eggs."

made a profit, which Scott believed it would, Carnegie would make a profit, too.

Carnegie didn't have any money saved for investments, so Scott loaned him the money. A few months later, Carnegie arrived at work to find a white envelope lying on his desk. It contained a check for ten dollars, the profit from his Adams Express investment. As Carnegie later recalled, "I shall remember that check as long as I live." It represented the first money he ever earned from an investment: "something that I had not worked for with the sweat of my brow. 'Eureka!' I cried. 'Here's the goose that lays the golden eggs.'"

The Pennsylvania Railroad promoted Thomas Scott to general superintendent in the fall of 1856. Carnegie moved with him to the company's central offices in Altoona. His new salary was fifty dollars a month. His mother, Margaret, and brother, Tom, stayed in Allegheny until they were able to rent out their house. They joined Carnegie in Altoona in the spring of 1857. In Altoona, Carnegie discovered a love for horseback riding. His favorite horse was a high-spirited stallion named Dash.

During the 1850s, railroad track in the United States increased in distance from nine thousand to more than thirty thousand miles. As this iron network grew, connecting all the states east of the Mississippi River, railroads improved in comfort and efficiency. In the mid-1850s, railroad car builder Theodore T. Woodruff invented a sleeping car.

Working long hours for low pay, immigrants provided much of the labor needed to lay thousands of miles of railroad track in the United States.

A railroad car containing beds and mattresses, the sleeping car allowed travelers to get a good night's sleep on long trips. Previously, train passengers had nowhere to sleep but in their chairs or on benches.

The Pennsylvania Railroad began placing Woodruff's sleeping cars on its trains. Carnegie, newly enthused about investing, purchased stock in the Woodruff Sleeping Car Company. He didn't have enough money to pay for the stock, so he worked out a monthly payment plan with the company. When the first payment of $217.50 came due, Carnegie once again found himself short on cash. He went to a local banker and applied for a loan. The huge banker, well over six feet tall, put his arm around Carnegie, who stood just five feet, three inches. The banker said he'd be glad to lend him the money. Within two years, Carnegie was earning nearly five thousand dollars a year from his Woodruff Sleeping Car Company stock. "Blessed be the man who invented sleep," Carnegie commented on the investment that proved to be the foundation of his great wealth.

In the fall of 1859, Thomas Scott became vice president of the Pennsylvania Railroad, with an office in Philadelphia. He asked twenty-four-year-old Carnegie if he thought he could handle the position of superintendent of the railroad's Western Division. Supremely self-confident, Carnegie assured Scott that he could. Thus Carnegie became head of one of the largest and most heavily traveled sections of railroad in the United States. He earned the incredible salary of fifteen hundred dollars a year.

By the mid-nineteenth century, Andrew Carnegie had risen to a position of leadership within the Pennsylvania Railroad.

FIVE

Railroads and War

1859–1861

The Pennsylvania Railroad officially announced Carnegie's promotion to superintendent on December 1, 1859. Carnegie promptly hired his sixteen-year-old brother, Tom, as his personal secretary and telegraph operator. He also hired the first female telegraph operator in the country, his cousin Maria Hogan.

Carnegie's new position required the family to move back to Pittsburgh. They had been away from the city's dirty air for three years, and the pollution bothered them more than ever when they returned. When they heard about a home available in the suburb of Homewood, they jumped at the chance to move. Carnegie purchased the modest two-story frame house, surrounded by Norway spruce and flowers.

A harsh winter followed his promotion. The constant freezing and thawing, combined with poorly constructed railroad tracks, caused frequent breaks in the railroad line. Carnegie recalled forty-seven breaks in one night. With so many breaks, train wrecks were common. As superintendent,

Carnegie was responsible for clearing the wrecks and keeping the trains moving. He worked nonstop, sometimes going days without sleep, and pushed his men as hard as he pushed himself. As he wrote in his autobiography, "I was probably the most inconsiderate superintendent that ever was entrusted with the management of a great property, for, never knowing fatigue myself, being kept up by a sense of responsibility probably, I overworked the men and was not careful enough in considering the limits of human endurance."

Carnegie's primary goal in managing the railroad was to keep traffic flowing, whatever the cost. He would have workers lay railroad track around train wrecks or burn wrecked freight cars that blocked the track. As superintendent, he rarely delegated authority, preferring to give orders himself. Once, when a serious accident derailed several freight cars, Carnegie bustled about the scene, barking out orders and directing workmen. A burly Irishman, not realizing the small young man was the boss, picked him up and placed him out of the way, saying, "Get out of me way, ye brat of a boy."

Although Carnegie spent a lot of time among rough railroad workers on the job, his Homewood neighbors were socially prominent. They invited him to dinner parties and other social gatherings. His quick intelligence, humor, and vitality made him a popular guest. He loved discussing the important issues of the day and always had something to say. At times, especially if someone expressed an idea that differed from his, he could be arrogant or boastful. Yet he was also charming and genial. His light blue eyes told the story. They could sparkle with mischief, fill with tears, or reveal a steely glint in a matter of moments.

As a poor immigrant boy, Carnegie had not had a refined upbringing. To keep up with his cultured and well-educated friends, he set out to improve his social skills. He began to pay strict attention to his language, taking night classes in French and elocution, or public speaking. Leila Addison, a highly educated and refined friend, corrected his grammar and pronunciation. He read and reread the English classics. He also learned the importance of good manners and tried to be gentle in tone, polite and courteous to all.

One frequent topic of conversation at social gatherings of this period concerned slavery, a practice that was threatening to bring the nation to the brink of civil war. The Northern states had already abolished, or outlawed, slavery, but the practice continued in the South. And Southern states were threatening to secede, or withdraw, from the United States, if slavery was outlawed nationwide.

PENNSYLVANIA SOCIETY

FOR

PROMOTING THE ABOLITION OF SLAVERY,

THE

RELIEF OF FREE NEGROES UNLAWFULLY HELD IN BONDAGE,

AND FOR

IMPROVING THE CONDITION OF THE AFRICAN RACE.

The title page from a report calling for the abolition (ending) of slavery. The issue of slavery divided the nation in the mid-1800s. Carnegie firmly sided with the abolitionists.

Andrew Carnegie detested slavery. The thought of owning another human being offended and disgusted him, and he reminded anyone who would listen that all men were born free and equal. He bombarded newspaper editors with his opinions, urging that slavery be abolished throughout the United States. In a letter to Dod in 1855, Carnegie wrote, "I am an enthusiastic & ultra abolitionist. . . . [Slavery] is the greatest evil in the world and I promise you that whatever influence I may acquire shall be used to overthrow it."

Several years later, in 1861, civil war did break out in the United States. Eleven Southern states seceded from the rest of the nation and formed the Confederate States of America. Fighting began with a Confederate attack on Fort Sumter, South Carolina, on April 12, 1861. The Northern states, or Union, mobilized for war.

The Confederate attack on Fort Sumter in 1861

Simon Cameron, the U.S. secretary of war, appointed Thomas Scott general manager of military railroads and telegraph lines. Both were critical for the war effort: railroads for the movement of troops and supplies, the telegraph to keep communication open to President Abraham Lincoln in the nation's capital, Washington, D.C. Scott moved to Washington and summoned Carnegie to act as his assistant.

Leaving his job with the Pennsylvania Railroad, Carnegie quickly assembled a small corps of railroad men and set out for the capital. Getting to Washington, however, proved difficult. Confederate sympathizers in Baltimore, Maryland, had destroyed railroad and telegraph lines to Washington, virtually cutting it off from the rest of the nation. As Southern troops advanced on the defenseless capital, President Lincoln waited anxiously for Union troops and supplies to arrive. Carnegie's first task, repairing damaged railroad tracks and telegraph lines, became the highest priority of the war.

Carnegie and his men bypassed Baltimore by taking a train to Perryville, Maryland, then a ferryboat to Annapolis. At Annapolis, they discovered that the short railroad line into Washington had also been destroyed. Carnegie, his railroad crew, and General Ben Butler's Eighth Massachusetts Regiment repaired the damaged track. On the morning of April 25, they boarded a train and began their trip to the capital.

Carnegie rode beside the engineer. Near the outskirts of Washington, he saw that the telegraph lines beside the railroad tracks had been pulled to the ground and pinned down with wooden stakes, cutting off telegraphic communication. Carnegie stopped the train, jumped off, and released the stakes. The freed wires struck him in the face, cutting a gash across his cheek. With blood dripping from his face, Carnegie and the desperately needed troops entered Washington.

Scott placed Carnegie in charge of railroads and tele-graphic communications in nearby Virginia. In early June, Carnegie established his headquarters in the Virginia city of Alexandria. He and his crew worked tirelessly. They rebuilt Long Bridge, a railroad bridge over the Potomac River, and had it ready for troop movement in seven days. They also built telegraph stations in Alexandria, Burke Station, and Fairfax, Virginia.

During the bloody Battle of Bull Run, which took place on July 21, 1861, Carnegie worked in the telegraph office at Burke Station, a village about five miles from the battlefield. He spent the day sending messages to Washington and load-ing trains with wounded soldiers. He was deeply moved by the horror of the war. In witnessing so much death and destruction, he developed a passion for world peace that would last a lifetime.

Union troops protect Long Bridge. Carnegie and his crews quickly rebuilt the crucial crossing after it sustained damage during battle.

Fierce fighting during the Battle of Bull Run, 1861. Carnegie was stationed a few miles from this first major land battle of the Civil War.

Shortly after Bull Run, Carnegie suffered sunstroke while supervising the repair of a railroad bridge. He returned to Washington to recover, where Scott, recently appointed assistant secretary of war, gave him a different job. Scott put Carnegie in charge of all military railroad and telegraph service. His office in the War Department building received all incoming telegraphs from the field of battle. President Lincoln visited the office frequently, following news of the fighting closely— practically living in the office when a battle was in progress. In this way, Carnegie got to know and respect the president. He called Lincoln "the greatest political genius of our era."

Still ill and worried that he might contract typhoid, a disease that was spreading near Washington, Carnegie moved home to Pittsburgh in September 1861. He resumed his position with the Pennsylvania Railroad. But he soon discovered that the railroad alone couldn't satisfy his restless spirit.

Oil wells along Oil Creek near Titusville, Pennsylvania, in the 1860s

SIX

A Little of This, A Little of That

1861–1865

As the Civil War continued to rage, Carnegie threw himself into his work for the railroad. He became an expert at tracking and reducing costs. He suggested increasing working hours for trainmen from ten to twelve or thirteen hours a day. With the longer workday, crews wouldn't need to be changed as often, and the railroad would save money on labor costs. He suggested lowering the price of train fares to attract more customers. He also urged railroad officials to keep telegraph stations open all night and to build a double track between Altoona and Pittsburgh. He worked hard, pushing himself beyond most men's endurance. The Pennsylvania Railroad's profits soared.

In the fall of 1861, large-scale oil drilling began ninety miles north of Pittsburgh along a small river called Oil Creek. Oil, or petroleum, was a valuable source of fuel. Oil was so valuable that people started calling it "liquid gold."

Carnegie took a steamboat much like one of these to investigate the oil fields at Oil Creek. The trip convinced him to buy stock in the growing oil business.

William Coleman, Carnegie's Homewood neighbor, had an opportunity to buy some prime land in the oil region. He wanted Carnegie to invest in the venture and persuaded Carnegie to accompany him to the isolated area in western Pennsylvania.

The two men took a steamboat up the Allegheny River to Oil City, a boomtown at the mouth of Oil Creek. From there, they traveled by wagon over primitive roads to the oil wells. They slept in shanties, surrounded by black, foul-smelling liquid gold. In the midst of the filth and confusion, a party atmosphere prevailed. Fortunes seemed within reach, and spirits were high.

The trip convinced Carnegie to invest in oil. He used his profits from the Woodruff Sleeping Car Company to purchase more than one thousand shares of stock in the Columbia Oil Company, Coleman's business. It proved to be a spectacular investment. Carnegie earned nearly eighteen thousand dollars in dividends—his share of the company's profits—the first year alone. With his oil, sleeping car, and Adams Express profits, Carnegie then invested in other companies, including the Western Union Telegraph Company, the Pennsylvania Oil Company, and the Freedom Iron Company.

The railroad business continued to grow, helped along in part by several laws passed by Congress. The Homestead Act, passed in 1862, offered free land in the West to any citizen who would farm it. The Pacific Railroad Act, also passed in 1862, authorized the Union Pacific and Central Pacific Railroads to construct rail lines across North America. The project was known as the transcontinental railroad.

A family of homesteaders on their way west for free land, 1860s

While the Civil War continued, few Americans were able to devote energy to westward expansion. But Carnegie realized that expansion would skyrocket after the war. He knew that railroad track would be in high demand and that railroad bridges would be needed to span the Ohio, Missouri, Mississippi, and rivers farther west.

During this era, railroad bridges were made of wood. As railroad superintendent, Carnegie saw that wooden bridges frequently caught fire from sparks created by passing trains. The bridges had to be replaced often. Jacob Linville, a bridge engineer for the Pennsylvania Railroad, had designed an iron bridge, which was fireproof. So Carnegie proposed forming a

Two early iron bridges in the United States. The bridges show different styles of construction: flat topped, foreground, *and arched,* background.

Iron bridges were in great demand during the 1860s. Competing bridge companies, such as the one advertised above, quickly entered the market along with Carnegie's Piper and Shiffler Company.

company to build iron bridges. Along with Linville, Thomas Scott, and bridge experts Aaron Shiffler and John Piper, Carnegie formed the Piper and Shiffler Company in early 1862. The business made money from the start.

In the spring of that year, Carnegie's habit of working too hard took its toll on his health. He became seriously ill for the first time in his life. He had never fully recovered from his sunstroke the year before, and hot weather drained his energy and left him weak. His doctors recommended rest, so in May 1862, Carnegie applied for a three-month leave of absence from his job. J. Edgar Thomson, president of the Pennsylvania Railroad, granted the leave, and Carnegie, his mother, and his friend Thomas Miller sailed for Dunfermline, Scotland, in late June.

On this, his first trip back to Dunfermline, Carnegie found his hometown smaller than he remembered it. He recognized a sharp contrast between the frightened boy who had left the town fourteen years earlier and the successful businessman who had returned. He planned to tour Britain and western Europe after visiting Dunfermline but had to abandon those plans when he caught a cold that developed into pneumonia. A Scottish doctor bled him, drawing blood from a vein in an effort to remove disease. But this treatment only made Carnegie weaker. He remained in bed in Dunfermline for six weeks, part of the time in critical condition. The illness put an end to the vacation, and as soon as Carnegie was well enough, the travelers returned to Pittsburgh.

A warm reception greeted Carnegie at home. As his train pulled into the station, Pennsylvania Railroad men shot off a burst of cannon fire to celebrate his return. Over the next several months, Carnegie regained his strength and resumed his responsibilities at the railroad.

Thomas Miller, the friend who had accompanied Carnegie and his mother to Scotland, was a partner in the firm of Kloman and Company. This small business made high-quality iron railroad axles. Miller asked Carnegie to help settle a long-running business dispute between the company partners. Carnegie reluctantly agreed, and the parties involved eventually reached a settlement. Not long afterward, however, fighting within the company began again, and the other partners forced Miller out. Carnegie thought Miller had been treated unfairly. So the two men decide to build their own iron mill, the Cyclops Iron Company, half a mile up the Allegheny River from the Kloman plant.

Carnegie's salary from the railroad amounted to twenty-four hundred dollars a year at this time. Yet because of his other businesses and investments, his yearly income was close to fifty thousand dollars. That was twice as much money as the president of the United States earned each year. One day, a friend dropped by and asked Carnegie how he was getting along. "I'm rich! I'm rich!" Carnegie answered.

Carnegie knew he could earn far more on his own than he could by working for someone else. But he considered his work for the railroad his contribution to the war effort. He decided to stay on until the war ended and then to resign.

The Civil War formally ended in April 1865. A few weeks before, on March 28, 1865, Carnegie resigned from the railroad. He was determined to make a fortune. In a letter to his cousin Dod, he shared his plan "to expand as my means do and ultimately to own a noble place in the country, cultivate the rarest flowers, the best breeds of cattle, own a magnificent lot of horses and be distinguished for taking the deepest interest in all those about my place."

General Lee, right, surrenders to General Grant, left, on April 9, 1865, officially bringing an end to the Civil War.

Union Pacific steam locomotives cross Devil's Gate Bridge in Utah during the construction of the transcontinental railroad. A symbol of unity, the project was followed with great fervor by many Americans.

SEVEN

Choosing a Specialty

1865–1874

After the Civil War, Americans were determined to unite the nation, not only the North with the South but also the East with the West. Railroads were the key to that unification. Construction on the transcontinental railroad had come to a standstill during the war. But when the conflict ended, completing the railroad became a national obsession. At the same time, hundreds of thousands of Americans took advantage of the Homestead Act, flocking westward to claim farms.

With all this movement west, orders for iron bridges poured into the Piper and Shiffler bridge company, which had only a small factory. The company couldn't handle the volume of orders, so Carnegie reorganized, adding new partners and money. The newly reorganized business was called the Keystone Bridge Company.

Carnegie realized that to maximize the success of the company, he needed a reliable and cheap source of iron beams and plates. He already had the Cyclops Iron Company, but he needed some talented businesspeople to run it.

To get that talent, Carnegie made a deal to merge Cyclops with its rival up the river, Kloman and Company, which had extremely capable managers.

Carnegie called the new company Union Iron Mills. He chose the name to commemorate the union of the former rival companies, as well as the reunification of the United States after the Civil War. As soon as the merger negotiations were complete, Carnegie set out for a nine-month tour of Europe. He left his twenty-two-year-old brother, Tom, in charge of his businesses.

In May 1865, Carnegie sailed on the steamer *Scotia* for a grand tour of Europe. He was accompanied by his friends Henry Phipps Jr. and John Vandevort. In Liverpool, England, an acquaintance named John Franks joined the party, and the group then toured Britain, France, Germany, Austria, and Italy. In describing Carnegie on this trip, Franks wrote in his travel diary, "As to health, this is so overflowing that it is extremely difficult to keep him within reasonable bounds, to restrain him within the limits of moderately orderly behavior, he is so continually mischievous and so exuberantly joyous."

Carnegie's boundless energy drove the group. They climbed mountains, attended operas, visited art galleries, and toured famous monuments. Each new experience thrilled him, and Carnegie's comment from Vienna was typical: "By golly boys, there's a great treat in store for us here."

Business concerns always occupied a corner of Carnegie's mind, however. While traipsing through Europe, he wrote a constant stream of letters to his brother, Tom. Sometimes he offered advice and questioned Tom in detail about his various business concerns. Other times, Carnegie thanked Tom profusely for his hard work. The travelers sailed for home in the spring of 1866.

Carnegie returned to the United States to find the nation gripped with railroad fever. As the transcontinental railroad cut through mountain passes and snaked across hundreds of miles of desert, Carnegie resolved to place Woodruff sleeping cars on the great Union Pacific line. He had a fierce competitor in reaching this goal: George Mortimer Pullman, whom Carnegie called "a lion in the path."

Carnegie owned a majority interest—more stock than any other investor—in the company that made Woodruff sleeping cars. Although the cars were popular, they contained three-tiered berths, which made for a crowded ride. Based in Chicago, railroad capital of the nation, George Pullman improved on Theodore Woodruff's design. He built a roomier sleeping car with just two tiers, then added luxury. Whereas Woodruff's cars were simple and unadorned, Pullman's sleeping cars contained elegant curtains, beautiful chandeliers, and lavish decorations. Newspapers called them "rolling palaces."

The luxurious interior of a Pullman sleeping car. Often called "rolling palaces," the cars included spacious sleeping areas, or berths, far left, ample seating room, right, and lavish decorations.

A shrewd businessman, Carnegie teamed up with competitor George Pullman, forming the Pullman Palace Car Company. The company's main factory in Illinois is shown above.

In 1867 the Union Pacific Railroad held a meeting in New York to decide which company's sleeping cars it would buy. Both Carnegie and Pullman attended the meeting and presented proposals. After the meeting, both men mounted the marble staircase of the St. Nicholas Hotel, and Carnegie struck up a conversation with Pullman. He pointed out that their rivalry benefited no one and suggested that their companies should merge. When Pullman asked what the new company would be called, Carnegie suggested the Pullman Palace Car Company. That idea settled the matter, for Carnegie knew that naming the company after Pullman expressed the highest form of flattery.

Carnegie arranged the merger because he didn't think he could beat Pullman. By merging, he would at least get a piece of the sleeping car business instead of nothing. The deal was signed with Union Pacific, and Pullman sleeping cars soon crisscrossed the nation. Carnegie had once again found a "golden egg."

In the summer of 1867, Tom Carnegie married Lucy Coleman, daughter of Carnegie's oil partner, William Coleman. Carnegie and his mother gave their Homewood house to the newlyweds and moved to New York City. They took up residence in the elegant St. Nicholas Hotel. Surrounded by fluted Corinthian columns, lofty ceilings, deep velvety carpeting, gilt-framed mirrors, and intricately woven tapestries, the Carnegies lived in splendor. Andrew opened an office at 19 Broad Street, where he ran his business concerns.

In December 1868, Carnegie sat at his desk at the St. Nicholas Hotel and scribbled out a list of his investments and the income he received from each one. His holdings in sixteen companies provided an annual income of $56,110. Most Americans at this time earned less than $500 per year.

But Carnegie's tremendous wealth pricked his conscience. He loved making money, and he loved spending it. Yet he felt guilty about loving money so much. He wrestled with the dilemma of how to make a lot of money yet also remain a good person who contributed to society in a meaningful way. In a memo accompanying his 1868 list, he wrote:

> Man must have an idol—The amassing of wealth is one of the worst species of [idol worship]. No idol more debasing than the worship of money. Whatever I engage in I must push inordinately therefor[e] should I be careful to choose that life which will be the most elevating in its character. To continue much longer overwhelmed by business cares and with most of my thoughts wholly upon the way to make more money in the shortest time, must degrade me beyond hope of permanent recovery.

He vowed to retire in two years, at age thirty-five, and to make no effort to raise his salary beyond fifty thousand dollars.

He also promised to distribute his excess income to worthy causes. But the lure of wealth proved too strong to ignore.

As railroads continued to grow, trains got longer and heavier. In addition to catching fire, wooden railroad bridges often collapsed under the weight of the trains. Iron bridges were in constant demand. Carnegie set out to make sure his Keystone Bridge Company built those new bridges. His friendship with J. Edgar Thomson and Thomas Scott of the Pennsylvania Railroad helped him secure business with other railroads. Before long, Keystone was one of the most prominent and profitable bridge builders in the nation.

Carnegie found bridge building intensely satisfying. With their great iron beams, cables, and stone pylons, Keystone bridges bound the country into one nation. Each bridge fed Carnegie's belief that he was building a beautiful and practical monument. Carnegie insisted that the company use the best materials and technology available to build bridges of superior quality. He set exacting standards for safety and told one of his clients, "We never have built and we never will build a cheap bridge. Ours don't fall."

In the spring of 1867, engineer James B. Eads had designed a bridge to cross the Mississippi River at St. Louis. His revolutionary design called for three arches of steel and iron: one 520 feet long and two others 502 feet long. They would be the largest arched spans in the world. The Keystone Company was hired to build the bridge.

Carnegie asked Jacob Linville, also an engineer, to review the plans for the bridge. Linville declared the bridge design unsafe and cautioned that the bridge would collapse under its own weight. But James Eads convinced Carnegie of the design's soundness, and construction began in the summer of 1868.

*Bridge designer and
mechanical engineer
James Buchanan Eads*

The bridge faced countless delays and problems. Workers found Eads difficult and demanding. At one point during the construction, Eads collapsed from overwork and left for Europe to recover. Work on the bridge stopped until he returned several months later.

Eads insisted on using steel to build certain parts of the bridge. A mixture of iron and carbon, steel was stronger and more durable than iron. It was also difficult to make and expensive. Until then, steel had been used for small items, such as needles, pocketknives, and watch springs. Eads demanded a quantity and quality of steel never before seen. He set precise standards for its strength and durability. Andrew Kloman of the Union Iron Works designed special machines for testing the steel. After repeated failures, the steel finally met Eads's approval.

Keystone completed the 1,627-foot bridge, called an engineering masterpiece by the press, in the spring of 1874.

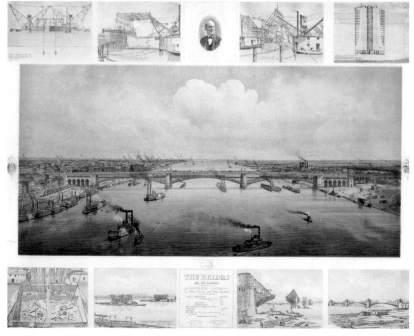

Steamships chug along the Mississippi River near the Eads Bridge at St. Louis, center. *The stages of bridge construction are shown,* top and bottom, *along with Eads's portrait,* top center.

It was finished three years behind schedule and at double the originally estimated cost. On July 4, 1874, more than three hundred thousand spectators stood in 102-degree heat and watched in awe as the first train rolled across the bridge. It seemed miraculous that such a graceful structure could support the heavy load.

The bridge clearly demonstrated the superiority of steel over iron. Not only bridges but also rails (railroad tracks), beams, plates, and other railroad equipment were stronger and longer lasting when made of steel. Carnegie quickly saw that steel would replace iron as the primary building material in the industrial United States. Several years earlier, the Pennsylvania

Railroad had begun buying steel rails from Great Britain. He also realized that if he didn't find a way to make steel rails himself, he'd lose his rail business to British companies.

He needed to find a way to make large quantities of steel inexpensively. A trip to England solved his dilemma. There, Carnegie toured a steel mill that used a new kind of furnace, the Bessemer converter, to turn iron into steel. Until that time, steel had been made in small batches. The converter, designed by a man named Henry Bessemer, made it possible to make high-quality steel by the ton. When Carnegie returned home, he began to concentrate his energies on one business: steel.

Filled with excitement, he decided to build a company to produce steel rails. He was joined in the venture by his iron company associates Phipps and Kloman; his brother, Tom; his old oil partner William Coleman; and David McCandless, a highly respected businessman. Carnegie called the new business Carnegie, McCandless and Company, supplying the largest amount of funding for the business himself. Describing this decision, Carnegie resolved "to put all good eggs in one basket and then watch that basket."

William Coleman found the perfect site for the new steel mill—one hundred acres of farmland twelve miles south of Pittsburgh on the Monongahela River. Called Braddock's Field, the location provided access to both the Pennsylvania and the Baltimore & Ohio Railroads, which Carnegie knew would be vital to his new business. The railroads would carry raw materials to the mill and finished products to customers.

Carnegie planned the new mill carefully. It would contain the best equipment and be built by the most talented engineers money could buy. He knew his major customer would be the Pennsylvania Railroad. So he named the mill the Edgar

Thomson Steel Works (called ET for short), after the president of the Pennsylvania Railroad. Lucy Furnaces, a kind of blast furnace Carnegie had built a few years earlier (named after Tom Carnegie's wife), would provide the mill with iron at low cost.

Shortly after construction began, the powerful banking house of Jay Cooke and Company failed and set off one of the worst depressions in American history. Massive unemployment spread across the nation. Businesses went bankrupt.

Nervous and confused investors gather near an investment office on New York's Wall Street during the economic crisis of the 1870s.

Those lucky enough to keep their jobs saw their wages plunge by 25 percent. It seemed like the worst time imaginable to start a new business.

Carnegie didn't panic. He recognized that depressions were temporary and predicted that when this one ended, the U.S. economy would be stronger than ever. He used the financial slump to snatch up equipment for low prices and workers for low wages. He sold some of his Pullman and Western Union stock and used the money to continue construction on his mill.

Carnegie made his first charitable gift at this time: twenty-five thousand dollars for the building of a public swimming pool in Dunfermline. He also donated an organ to the church his father had attended in Allegheny. He had vowed in 1868 to retire in 1870 and start giving away his wealth. Now, in 1874, he had finally begun to make charitable gifts, but he was a long way from retirement.

A piece of Carnegie's growing empire, the Edgar Thomson Steel Works, above, *was one of the best steel mills of the era.*

EIGHT

Building an Empire
1874–1889

Alexander Holley, the foremost authority on Bessemer steel in America, designed the Edgar Thomson Steel Works. He improved on Henry Bessemer's basic mill design and created for Carnegie the most technologically advanced steel mill of its day.

Carnegie, who had a knack for picking staff of exceptional talent, hired the best steel men he could find to run ET. He chose William Jones, recommended by Holley, as ET's general superintendent. Jones, considered a mechanical genius, had started working in iron mills at age ten. By the time he came to work for Carnegie, he knew every phase of the steel-making process firsthand. He also brought to ET a workforce of more than two hundred experienced workers.

Many of the workers were members of a labor union called the Sons of Vulcan. Like other labor unions, this group of workers banded together to negotiate with employers over issues such as pay and working conditions. Some American unions grew large and powerful. But the Sons of Vulcan, a small ironworkers union, wasn't very strong.

ET began production in August 1875, with an order for two thousand steel rails from the Pennsylvania Railroad. Most of the steel during this period was used to make railroad track. With Carnegie's railroad contacts, he had a distinct advantage over his competitors in the steel business. Carnegie steel also went into construction of the Washington Monument in Washington, D.C., the elevated railroads in New York and Chicago, and the exhibition buildings for the Centennial Exposition in Philadelphia—a large festival celebrating the nation's hundredth birthday in 1876. Profits soared, and when Carnegie received ET's first six-month financial report in April 1876, he exclaimed, "Where is there such a business!"

Carnegie structured his steel business as a partnership. Each partner contributed his business talent, as well as his money, and actively participated in the operation of the company. Each partner managed a specific department, such as blast furnace operations or shipping, while Carnegie supervised the whole company and marketed the steel. Carnegie had invested the most money in the business, so when disagreements arose among the partners, his opinion always prevailed.

Carnegie never passed up an opportunity to make a sale. He even promoted his steel at social gatherings. Satisfied customers wrote testimonials, declarations praising the business, which Carnegie then sent to railroad presidents along with letters asking for orders. He gave frequent interviews to reporters, always pushing his steel rails as the "best in the world."

He followed a business philosophy he had learned while working for the Pennsylvania Railroad: keep production high and costs low. He knew what it cost to run each department down to the penny and constantly searched for ways to lower costs. "Watch the costs and the profits will take care of themselves" became Carnegie's constant refrain.

A Bessemer converter "blows" steel. Air blown into the converter meets flame, superheating and purifying iron to produce steel. Carnegie enjoyed watching the steel-making process.

He was a hands-on boss, often visiting the factory floor. He loved watching the roaring flames that rushed from the Bessemer converter. He kept a sharp eye on production. If a department fell behind in the quality or quantity of steel produced, Carnegie sent William Jones to investigate. He also closely watched his managers, analyzing each one's performance and noting who produced the best results. He called some of his managers "young geniuses," gave them more and more responsibility, and sat back to see how they handled the pressure. If a "young genius" succeeded, Carnegie made him a partner, giving him a small share of ownership of the company. If the man failed, Carnegie forced him out of his job. As he explained, "If he can win the race he is our race horse and if he can't he goes to the cart."

One of Carnegie's "young geniuses," seventeen-year-old Charles Schwab, began work at Edgar Thomson as a stake driver, earning a dollar a day. After six months, Carnegie put Schwab in charge of construction of a new blast furnace. He rose quickly through the ranks and became one of Carnegie's most valued managers.

But Carnegie's generosity to his managers didn't filter down to his ordinary laborers. The men worked twelve-hour days, seven days a week. The Fourth of July was their only holiday. According to one mill worker, "I lost forty pounds the first three months I came into this business. It sweats the life out of a man." Another worker said,

These steelworkers are collecting molten, or melted, steel for molding. Steel is formed into beams, rails, and many other items before it cools and hardens.

"It drags you down mentally and morally, just as it does physically." Carnegie paid standard steel industry wages, which were barely above the poverty level. He believed that any worker who wished to raise himself to a higher position had every opportunity to do so, just as Charles Schwab had done.

In October 1878, Carnegie took another overseas vacation, departing from San Francisco, California. From there he and his friend John Vandevort stepped aboard the S.S. *Belgic* for a trip around the world. He and "Vandy" traveled west to Japan, China, Hong Kong, Singapore, India, Egypt, and Europe. The trip broadened Carnegie's intellectual outlook. During his travels, he reflected on the human race as a whole and felt connected to the people of each country he visited. He saw stark poverty, yet he believed that each nation was progressing. "If all is not well," he wrote, "yet all is coming well. In this faith we find peace."

By 1880 Carnegie was forty-five years old and still unmarried. He had dated many women but chose not to marry during his mother's lifetime. Mother and son were extremely close. She depended on him, and he doted on her. He felt it was his duty to take care of her, just as she had taken care of him as a child.

That year, Carnegie began dating twenty-three-year-old Louise Whitfield. The daughter of a wealthy merchant, Louise was a quiet, serious-minded young woman. Taller than Carnegie by about three inches, she captivated him with her grace and dignity. Like Carnegie, she enjoyed horseback riding. The couple frequently rode together in New York's Central Park. She quickly became Carnegie's favorite riding partner. The couple grew close, but they did not discuss marriage.

Carnegie remained focused on business. By 1881 ET was manufacturing more steel rails than any of its rivals in Great Britain or America, yet Carnegie relentlessly pushed for more business. When a manager telegraphed that ET had broken all records for making steel one week, Carnegie questioned why the company wasn't breaking records every week.

To make his steel business more efficient, he combined the Edgar Thomson Steel Works, the Union Iron Mills, and several blast furnaces into one new company. Called Carnegie Brothers & Company, it was the largest steel company in the United States. Carnegie owned 55 percent of the business and appointed his brother, Tom, chairman of the board.

Shortly after this reorganization, Carnegie took his mother on his long-before promised trip to Dunfermline. They traveled with a group of close friends that Carnegie dubbed "the Gay Charioteers." The Charioteers spent seven weeks traveling leisurely from Brighton, in southern England, to Inverness in northern Scotland. They picnicked beside gentle streams, rested in thatch-roofed inns, and strolled over England's flowery countryside. When the Charioteers crossed the border into Scotland, Carnegie stopped the carriage and exclaimed, "O Scotland, my own, my native land, your exiled son returns with love for you as ardent as ever warmed the heart of man for his country." In Dunfermline, Carnegie donated a public library to the town—the first library he ever funded.

Back home that fall, Carnegie met industrialist Henry Clay Frick, a wealthy young entrepreneur, or businessman. Frick controlled 80 percent of the coal in Connellsville, Pennsylvania, a rich coal-producing region south of Pittsburgh. There, Frick baked coal into cakes called coke, a key ingredient in making steel. In December, Carnegie invited Frick

Coal industrialist and Carnegie partner Henry Clay Frick

and his wife to dine with Carnegie and his mother at the Windsor Hotel in New York. Carnegie entertained the party with stories of his recent coaching trip. His ready wit contrasted sharply with Frick's silent and frosty disposition. At the end of the dinner, Carnegie raised his glass and toasted Frick and a future Frick-Carnegie partnership.

Within a month, that partnership became a reality. Carnegie purchased stock in the Henry Clay Frick Coke Company. The alliance provided a guaranteed supply of coke for Carnegie's steel mill. More important, in Frick, Carnegie had found a strong partner who would help build his fortune.

The success of Carnegie's Edgar Thomson Steel Mill brought competition. A rival mill called the Homestead Steel Works opened one mile down the Monongahela River. Built with the latest technical advances of its day, Homestead contained the most modern equipment available. But labor problems plagued Homestead from the start.

A large portion of the Homestead workers belonged to the Amalgamated Association of Iron and Steel Workers, one of the most powerful labor unions in the country. Unlike the Sons of Vulcan at ET, the Homestead union was highly organized, well disciplined, and powerful. The union and Homestead's management clashed, and all the workers went on strike. They refused to work until their labor demands were met. When the market for steel rails fell, Homestead's management decided to sell the business.

Carnegie leaped at the chance to obtain a modern mill. In October 1883, he scooped up Homestead at a bargain price. He organized a new company, Carnegie, Phipps and Company, which included Homestead and the Lucy Furnaces.

Building his steel empire, Carnegie acquired the Homestead Steel Works, above, *in 1883.*

The Home Insurance Building in Chicago. Carnegie steel beams and girders made the construction of this first skyscraper possible.

He owned the majority interest in two complete and separate steel companies: Carnegie Brothers, and Carnegie, Phipps.

Although the demand for steel rails had fallen, sales increased for steel beams and girders, which were needed to build tall office buildings. Carnegie remodeled Homestead to make these beams, providing the steel for the country's first skyscraper, the ten-story Home Insurance Building, built in Chicago, Illinois, in 1885. Carnegie's factories also supplied steel for ships, farming equipment, barbed wire, pipelines, typewriters, bicycles, and other machines.

Carnegie's steel empire grew, and he poured the profits back into his companies. He updated equipment and constantly improved production. If a new machine could cut down the cost of making steel, even by as little as fifty cents per ton, he tore out and replaced old machinery. His partners often balked at this policy. They didn't want all the companies' profits put back into the businesses. The partners wanted dividends to spend as they pleased. But since Carnegie owned the majority interest in both firms, he won the debate. The more money his businesses made, the more he reinvested in plant expansion and improvement.

In steel manufacturing, Carnegie had more than enough to keep him busy. Yet during this time of business growth, a new career blossomed. Carnegie became a writer. He had always been a prolific letter writer, corresponding with friends, relatives, and newspaper editors. Now he began writing books and magazine articles. "If any man wants *bona fide* substantial power and influence in this world," Carnegie wrote, "he must handle the pen—that's flat. Truly, it is a nobler weapon than the sword, and a much nobler one than the tongue, both of which have nearly had their day."

Carnegie's first published work was *An American Four-in-Hand in Britain,* the travel diary of his carriage trip through England and Scotland, published by Charles Scribner's Sons in 1883. The book sold well, and the publisher reprinted it eighteen times over the next few years. Carnegie's first magazine article, "As Others See Us," appeared in the prestigious English periodical *Fortnightly Review.* In 1884 Scribner's published Carnegie's second book, *Round the World,* an account of his transglobal trip.

Much of Carnegie's writing dealt with politics and economics. He despised the British system of nobility, in which people inherited titles such as duke and earl. These people led lives of wealth, power, and privilege, not because of hard work but simply by being born into nobility. Carnegie loved his homeland, but he detested the British class system. "An aristocracy founded upon learning, and composed of those who know the most, is an institution with which we have no serious quarrel," he wrote. "It is claims from birth which make my blood boil." Carnegie believed that all people, regardless of background, should have an equal chance in life.

Carnegie believed that the United States, with its elected officials, had the perfect form of government. Because of his nonstop praise for the nation, Scotch novelist William Black called Carnegie the "Star-Spangled Scotchman."

Author William Black, right, *nicknamed Carnegie the "Star-Spangled Scotchman." The nickname poked fun at Carnegie's dual Scottish-American nationality and his deep appreciation of U.S. democracy.*

Queen Victoria, seated, center, *surrounded by other members
of the the British royal family in the late nineteenth century.
Carnegie's admiration of American democracy was equaled
by his great dislike of the British monarchy.*

In 1884 Carnegie funded a group of British newspapers, with
the goal of abolishing the British monarchy (government led
by a king or queen) and creating a republic—a nation in which
leaders were elected, not born, into office. Through the newspapers, Carnegie tirelessly preached his radical message.

The newspapers consistently lost money, so in 1885
Carnegie sold his interest in the papers. But he maintained his
burning desire to change Great Britain's form of government.

He wrote, "I would destroy, if I had the power, every vestige of privilege in England, and give to every man as man equal and exact privileges; but, at the same time, I would not shed a drop of blood, nor violate a law, nor use violence in any form, to bring about what I so much desire."

Carnegie's third book, *Triumphant Democracy* (1886), expressed his love for both his adopted country, the United States, and the land of his birth, Great Britain. But it also argued that democracy, the kind of government practiced in the United States, was the best form of government and that it made nations stronger. The book opens: "The old nations of the earth creep on at a snail's pace; the Republic [the United States] thunders past with the rush of the express."

Carnegie continued for more than five hundred pages praising the virtues of the United States. He urged England and other nations to eliminate their kings, queens, and lords and to establish presidents, congresses, and supreme courts. "The Republic may not give wealth, or happiness," Carnegie wrote, "she has not promised these, it is the freedom to pursue these, not their realization, which the Declaration of Independence claims." *Triumphant Democracy* created a sensation, selling more than thirty thousand copies in the United States and forty thousand in England. Translated into French and German, it sold well all over Europe. Carnegie considered the book his greatest achievement as a writer.

Despite his busy schedule, Carnegie and his mother retreated to a cottage in Cresson, Pennsylvania, in the Allegheny Mountains, from June to October each year. Ever since his sunstroke, Carnegie had been extremely sensitive to heat. He looked forward to the cool, pure mountain air, the wooded mountain trails, and his roomy Victorian Gothic house, perched on the highest hill in Cresson.

In the summer of 1886, Louise Whitfield visited Carnegie at Cresson. By then, their relationship had grown serious, but Carnegie was still not ready for marriage. That soon changed. In the fall of that year, Carnegie's brother, Tom, then forty-three years old, became ill and died, leaving a wife and nine children. Carnegie's mother then suffered from pneumonia, and Carnegie contracted typhoid fever.

In November, while he lay with fever in a semiconscious state, his mother died. Fearing Carnegie's reaction to the news of her death, his staff didn't tell him until a week later. In his grief, Carnegie sold the cottage at Cresson and packed away all pictures and mementos of his mother. For many years, he would not even mention her name.

With his mother gone, Carnegie's thoughts immediately turned to Louise. Now they could marry. As Carnegie slowly recuperated from typhoid, the couple began planning their wedding. On April 22, 1887, fifty-one-year-old Andrew Carnegie married thirty-year-old Louise Whitfield in front

The S.S. Fulda *carried Carnegie and his wife, Louise, to Britain for their honeymoon in 1887.*

of thirty friends and relatives. As a wedding gift, Carnegie presented his wife with a house in New York. Then the couple boarded the steamship S.S. *Fulda* for a honeymoon in England and Scotland.

Louise fell in love with the rugged beauty of her husband's homeland. The couple soon developed a routine, living in New York during the winter and in Scotland from May through October. They would continue this half-year pattern for the next twenty-seven years.

An impoverished immigrant family sits among drying laundry in their attic home. Sparse conditions were common to many nineteenth-century immigrants and working-class Americans.

NINE

War at Homestead

1889–1892

Andrew Carnegie made his fortune during the Gilded Age. In this era, the 1870s through about the early 1900s, industrialists such as Carnegie achieved greater wealth than anyone had ever seen before. Many of them celebrated and displayed their wealth by throwing lavish parties, building gaudy mansions, and collecting expensive artwork.

Contrasting this extreme wealth enjoyed by the few, however, was the poverty of the masses. As the industrialists were growing rich, millions of new immigrants were arriving in the United States from Europe. The newcomers were usually penniless. They took any jobs they could find, often working long hours in mills and factories for low pay. As more destitute immigrants arrived, tenements spread throughout eastern cities. The poor resented the rich and their gaudy displays of wealth.

Carnegie, a multimillionaire by the 1880s, also opposed lavish living and extravagance. Still, he argued that the great wealth of the few was good for the nation—as long as millionaires like himself distributed their excess wealth for the common good.

Though Carnegie claimed that he opposed lavish living, he owned two stately homes, including this one.

In June 1889, the *North American Review* published Carnegie's best-known and most successful work, "Wealth," later reprinted as "The Gospel of Wealth." In this article, Carnegie analyzed the problem of excess wealth and examined three possible ways for a millionaire to distribute that wealth.

The first method Carnegie described was to leave large sums to one's heirs—children and other relatives. Carnegie blasted this method as harmful to the recipients' moral and emotional fiber. He wrote, "Great sums bequeathed often work more for the injury than for the good of the recipients." He felt that receiving vast sums of money without having

NORTH AMERICAN REVIEW.

No. CCCXCL

JUNE, 1889.

WEALTH.

BY ANDREW CARNEGIE.

THE problem of our age is the proper administration of wealth, so that the ties of brotherhood may still bind together the rich and poor in harmonious relationship. The conditions of human life have not only been changed, but revolutionized, within the past few hundred years. In former days there was little difference between the dwelling, dress, food, and environment of the chief and those of his retainers. The Indians are to-day where civilized man then was. When visiting the Sioux, I was led to the wigwam of the chief. It was just like the others in external appearance, and even within the difference was trifling between it and those of the poorest of his braves. The contrast between the palace of the millionaire and the cottage of the laborer with us to-day measures the change which has come with civilization.

This change, however, is not to be deplored, but welcomed as highly beneficial. It is well, nay, essential for the progress of the race, that the houses of some should be homes for all that is highest and best in literature and the arts, and for all the refinements of civilization, rather than that none should be so. Much better this great irregularity than universal squalor. Without wealth there can be no Mæcenas. The "good old times" were not good old times. Neither master nor servant was as well situated then as to-day. A relapse to old conditions would be disastrous to both—not the least so to him who serves—and would sweep away civilization with it. But whether the change be for

VOL. CXLVIII.—NO. 391.   42

An excerpt from Carnegie's "Wealth," which appeared in the June 1889 issue of North American Review

worked for it deadened the talents and energies of heirs and resulted in their leading useless, unproductive lives.

The second method was to leave wealth to charity at death. Carnegie held no respect for this approach either, saying, "Men who leave vast sums in this way may fairly be thought men who would not have left it at all had they been able to take it with them." Carnegie thought this method was simply lazy.

Carnegie preferred a third method of disposing of wealth: distributing it during the owner's lifetime. He urged the millionaire to "consider all surplus revenues which come to him simply as trust funds, which he is called upon to administer."

In other words, the millionaire was to manage the money and see that it was put to good use. Carnegie explained that wealthy people needed to use the same talents with which they had amassed fortunes to distribute those fortunes for the common good. To those who left behind extra wealth, he wrote, "The man who dies thus rich dies disgraced."

At the time the article appeared, Carnegie had given only a swimming pool and a library to Dunfermline, a library to Braddock, Pennsylvania, an organ to a church in Allegheny, and six thousand dollars to the Western University of Pennsylvania. But after writing the article, Carnegie made frequent gifts. He donated libraries, church organs, and music halls on a regular basis. With funding from Carnegie, construction began on Carnegie Hall, the renowned music hall in New York City, in the spring of 1890.

In the summer of 1890, Carnegie acquired Duquesne Steel Works, a rival steel mill five miles up the Monongahela River from Homestead. Two years later, he merged all his steel businesses into one company, Carnegie Steel, the largest steel company in the world. Carnegie owned the majority interest in the huge firm and placed Henry Clay Frick in charge of its operation.

The new company immediately faced a fierce battle with its labor force at Homestead. Workers there, many of them members of the powerful Amalgamated Association of Iron and Steel Workers, were unhappy with their wages. They were demanding changes to their labor contract.

Carnegie had always been hard on his workers, driving them for long hours at low pay. At the same time, he had tried to establish himself as a friend of labor via two articles written for *Forum* magazine in 1886. "The right of the workingmen to combine and to form trades-unions is no less sacred

Steelworkers gather to listen to a labor leader, raised, center, *and to discuss striking for better wages. Carnegie believed in the workers' right to organize. His partners did not.*

than the right of the manufacturer to enter into associations and conferences with his fellows," he said in the first article. In the second article, he argued against hiring scab, or replacement, workers during a labor strike. Often during a strike, when regular employees refused to work, employers hired scabs to keep their plants running anyway. Carnegie criticized this tactic.

Labor leaders had applauded the *Forum* articles, believing that Carnegie supported their cause. But Henry Clay Frick and the rest of Carnegie's partners were embarrassed by the articles. They viewed labor as just one ingredient in the process of producing steel—an ingredient to be obtained at the lowest possible cost. Carnegie, it seemed, wanted it both ways. He wanted to lower labor costs *and* to appear before the world as a big-hearted, pro-labor employer, loved by one and all.

The labor contract at Homestead was due to expire on June 30, 1892. Management expected the workers to strike when the contract expired. But Carnegie did not think the striking workers would cause serious trouble. He did not want to bring in scabs or use any type of force against the strikers. He thought the mill would simply shut down during the strike until a settlement could be reached. So he left for his typical summer holiday, this year at Rannoch Lodge, an out-of-the-way cottage in the Highlands of Scotland. He left Frick in charge of Homestead, with instructions to handle the strike.

Frick decided to face the strike head-on. He prepared for war. To protect the mill from angry strikers, he ordered construction of a twelve-foot fence around the property, topped with barbed wire. He hired three hundred guards from the Pinkerton Detective Agency to defend the mill. Then he hired strikebreakers—scab workers to replace the strikers. On June 29, 3,800 Homestead workers went on strike. Calling the mill "Fort Frick," the strikers set up round-the-clock guards to prevent Frick from bringing in scabs.

On the morning of July 6, the three hundred Pinkerton guards hired to protect the mill floated up the Monongahela River on a barge. More than five thousand workers and their family members lined the riverbank to meet them. No one knows who fired the first shot, but a fierce battle raged for

Growing tension between labor and management erupted in the Homestead strike of 1892. Striking workers battled Pinkerton agents to prevent scab workers from taking their jobs.

twelve hours. The Pinkertons fired Winchester rifles. The workers blasted shotguns, Civil War muskets, a cannon, and dynamite. The Pinkertons raised a white flag four times to surrender, and four times the workers shot it down. At 5 P.M. the workers finally accepted the Pinkertons' surrender. But they still brutally beat the surrendering guards as they came ashore from the barge.

The Homestead battle left ten men dead and hundreds wounded. In the end, Pennsylvania governor Robert Pattison sent eight thousand National Guard troops to Homestead to restore order. Though out of the country, Andrew Carnegie faced a lot of criticism for his part in the tragedy. Most people believed he could have stepped in and settled the strike. But he chose to proceed with his vacation. "Carnegie's published works contained many platitudes [hollow remarks] about the rights of workingmen to organize," one newspaper reported, "but actions speak to the workmen at Homestead very much louder than words." Carnegie's inaction during the strike condemned him in the public eye and cast doubt on his sincerity.

Frick, meanwhile, bore the brunt of the conflict. On July 23, a Lithuanian immigrant named Alexander Berkman, a fanatic who identified with the workers but had no ties to the union, burst into Frick's office. Berkman shot Frick twice with

Labor sympathizer Alexander Berkman in 1892. Acting on his own, Berkman attempted to kill Henry Clay Frick.

a pistol at close range. When the bullets failed to kill Frick, Berkman pulled out a knife and stabbed Frick three times.

Frick recovered from his wounds, but the incident turned public opinion even more fiercely against Carnegie. "Three months ago Andrew Carnegie was a man to be envied," wrote the *St. Louis Post-Dispatch*. "To-day he is an object of mingled pity and contempt. . . . Say what you will of Frick, he is a brave man. Say what you will of Carnegie, he is a coward. And gods and men hate cowards."

By mid-August, Homestead was operating with seven hundred strikebreakers and the employees who had not participated in the strike. Carnegie never hired another union worker, and he never again trusted Frick. Although Frick remained at the head of Carnegie Steel, the two men grew more and more distant and distrustful of one another. Eventually, Carnegie forced Frick out of the company.

The Homestead strike and the public scorn that followed marked the lowest point in Andrew Carnegie's business career. "Nothing I have ever had to meet in all my life, before or since, wounded me so deeply," he wrote. The tragedy convinced Carnegie to assert stronger control over his companies and to repair the damage to his reputation.

*A confident and financially secure Carnegie at the turn of the
twentieth century*

TEN

The Richest Man in the World

1893–1901

After the Homestead strike, Carnegie set out to turn Carnegie Steel into the best steel company in the world. He held no official title in the company, but with 55 percent ownership, he had the final authority in its operation. He insisted on receiving detailed minutes from board of directors meetings, including notes on every discussion, decision, and comment made by each partner. He continually reminded his partners to lower costs, increase production, and charge less than their competitors.

His strategy focused on controlling all aspects of the steel-making process, from obtaining raw materials to the manufacturing of finished products. He had begun securing raw materials when he joined forces with Henry Clay Frick's coke empire. Next he concentrated on finding a guaranteed source of iron. This search led to an alliance with John D. Rockefeller, an oil tycoon with a variety of additional business interests, including railroads and shipping.

*John D. Rockefeller
controlled vast iron
resources. Carnegie and
Rockefeller struck up a
partnership that ensured
a steady supply of iron,
steel, and profits.*

Rockefeller owned a large portion of the Mesabi Range, a 120-mile strip of high-quality iron deposits in the hills of northern Minnesota. By 1896 the press eagerly looked forward to a Carnegie-Rockefeller battle, for it seemed likely that Rockefeller would build a steel mill. Instead, the two men reached an agreement. Carnegie agreed to lease Rockefeller's iron deposits and to ship the iron using Rockefeller's railroads and steamships. Both men got what they wanted: Carnegie got a huge supply of iron at a low price, and Rockefeller got a steady customer for his railroads and boats.

At home the Carnegies welcomed a new addition to the household in 1897. On March 30, forty-year-old Louise gave birth to their daughter, Margaret, named after Carnegie's mother. Sixty-one-year-old Andrew was thrilled to become a proud papa. For ten years, he and Louise had leased Cluny Castle, located in the central Highlands of Scotland, as their summer home. Shortly after Margaret's birth, Louise asked Andrew for a permanent summer home. She wanted the family to come and go as they pleased, instead of working around an owner's schedule. Carnegie immediately agreed to Louise's one condition: the new home had to be in the Highlands of Scotland.

Carnegie tried to buy Cluny Castle, but the owner refused to sell his ancestral home. So Carnegie began a search for another residence. It had to be large enough to accommodate the constant stream of visitors who descended on the Carnegies each summer. He insisted that the property contain a view of the sea, a trout stream, and a waterfall.

On a touring trip, Carnegie found Skibo Castle in the northeast corner of Scotland. The ancient castle needed massive repairs. But Louise and Andrew undertook the project with relish. They planned each detail with loving care, hiring workers and spending more than one million dollars over the next three years on improvements. They added eleven bedroom suites, five smaller bedrooms, a playroom, and fifteen bedrooms for servants. They added eighteen thousand acres to the original estate and built three lakes and a waterfall. A library, paneled in light oak with a pale yellow molded ceiling, contained twelve-foot built-in bookcases holding more than eight thousand volumes. A flag of Carnegie's own design fluttered from the highest turret: the Union Jack (British flag) and the American Stars and Stripes sewn together.

As construction progressed at Skibo, the Carnegies decided to build a home in New York City as well. They purchased a large tract of land at the corner of Ninety-first Street and Fifth Avenue and began building a sixty-four room, six-story home. A large garden surrounded the mansion, which contained the most modern features of the day: a structural steel frame, an elevator, and central heating and air-conditioning. Carnegie instructed the builders to carve his favorite slogans around the walls of the home's magnificent library. The slogans included: "Thine own reproach alone do fear," "The aids to a noble life are all within," and "All is well since all grows better."

The completed Carnegie mansion in New York, New York. The sixty-four-room home cost $1.5 million to construct, a staggering sum for the period.

The Battle at Cavite (Manila Bay) in the Philippine Islands during the Spanish-American War. A U.S. victory in the war led to U.S. occupation of the Philippines, which Carnegie opposed.

Never short on political opinions, Carnegie voiced strong opposition to U.S. policy in 1898, at the end of the Spanish-American War. Under the treaty ending the war with Spain, the United States agreed to pay $20 million to Spain for the Philippines, a group of islands off the southeast coast of Asia. The Philippines would become an American possession, land governed by the United States.

The treaty outraged Carnegie, who couldn't believe his beloved republic would stoop to buying a foreign country. He believed that the Philippine people should establish their own government. He even offered to pay President William McKinley $20 million for the island country so that he could give the people their freedom.

His offer ignored, Carnegie reacted in typical fashion, bombarding newspapers, magazines, and political officials with reasons why the Senate should not ratify the peace treaty with Spain. In a magazine article he wrote, "The Philippines have about seven and a half millions of people, composed of races bitterly hostile to one another, alien races, ignorant of our language and institutions. Americans cannot be grown there."

To Secretary of State John Hay, Carnegie wrote, "It is a great strain which the President is putting upon the loyalty of his friends and supporters. Many are bearing it—it has proved too great for me." In spite of Carnegie's efforts, the Senate approved the peace treaty.

Secretary of State John Hay at his desk. Carnegie wrote to Hay, attempting to stop the U.S. purchase of the Philippines.

Management and employees of Carnegie Steel and their families at a company picnic. By 1900 Carnegie employed thousands.

By 1900 Carnegie Steel Company, which included three complete steel mills—Edgar Thomson, Homestead, and Duquesne—plus Keystone Bridge, Union Iron, and several Lucy Furnaces, employed more than twenty thousand people. Carnegie Steel produced more steel than all the steel companies of Great Britain combined, and annual profits totaled $40 million.

In December of that year, Charles Schwab, who by then had worked his way up to president of Carnegie Steel, met with American banker and businessman J. P. Morgan. An international banker, Morgan was the king of high finance. He was interested in buying Carnegie's empire and asked Schwab to find Carnegie's price. Unsure how to approach Carnegie, Schwab visited Louise and asked her advice. Louise, anxious for her husband to retire, suggested that Schwab broach the subject after a game of golf.

International banker and financier J. P. Morgan. In 1900 Morgan showed a keen interest in buying the Carnegie empire.

Schwab purposely lost the golf game to put Carnegie in a good mood. Over lunch Schwab told Carnegie about Morgan's interest in Carnegie Steel. Sixty-five-year-old Carnegie felt torn. Part of him wanted to retire and start practicing what he preached in his "The Gospel of Wealth." The other part envisioned the power of his company in the coming years and the thrill of running such a vast business empire.

Carnegie told Schwab to let him sleep on the decision. When Schwab arrived the next morning, Carnegie handed him a scrap of paper with his price. Morgan could have Carnegie Steel for $480 million, equivalent to more than $10 billion in early twenty-first-century dollars. Schwab took the offer to Morgan, who glanced at it and immediately accepted the price.

Carnegie's share of the sale, after his partners had been paid their portions, amounted to $300 million. A few days after the agreement was made, Morgan visited Carnegie, shook his hand, and said, "Mr. Carnegie, I want to congratulate you on being the richest man in the world."

Andrew Carnegie had finally retired from business. Now people across the nation wondered whether he would follow his gospel of wealth and give his money away.

One of the richest men in the world, Carnegie felt obligated to give his wealth to others.

ELEVEN

Scientific Philanthropy
1901–1919

When Andrew Carnegie retired, he had already dabbled in philanthropy—charity meant to help people—giving more than $16 million worth of libraries, church organs, swimming pools, and music halls to cities and organizations. After retirement he began to practice what he called "scientific philanthropy." He analyzed potential donations, choosing those he felt would be of greatest benefit to humankind.

His main goal was to help those who would help themselves. "There is only one source of true blessedness in wealth, and that comes from giving it away for ends that tend to elevate our brothers and enable them to share it with us," he wrote. Louise enthusiastically supported her husband.

Libraries became Carnegie's specialty. He believed that literature provided a great benefit to people by building their intelligence and character. He encouraged children to read and said that "the really precious things of this world are its books."

Carnegie donated libraries with businesslike efficiency. A town council would apply for a library, locate a site, and agree to provide the books, staff, and maintenance. Carnegie then provided the building. He asked that the words "Let There Be Light" and the image of the rising sun be placed over the library's entrance. Over the course of his lifetime, Carnegie paid for 2,811 public libraries around the world at a cost of more than $50 million.

Most of Carnegie's gifts went toward education. He established the Carnegie Trust for the Universities of Scotland to pay the tuition of deserving poor students and to

A Carnegie library in Montgomery, Alabama, built in the early twentieth century. Carnegie funded many library buildings throughout the United States.

The Carnegie Technical Institute (Carnegie Mellon University) in the early twentieth century. The school remains a center for higher education.

improve scientific study and research at Scottish universities. He provided the funds to create a technical school in Pittsburgh, now called Carnegie Mellon University. He established the Carnegie Institution of Washington, dedicated to furthering scientific knowledge in the United States. Often in collaboration with universities, the institution set up research departments in scientific fields, including marine biology, anthropology, and astronomy. Carnegie was particularly proud of one Carnegie Institution project, the Mount Wilson Observatory in southern California, where new stars were discovered. Another institution-funded discovery tickled him, the fossil remains of an herbivorous dinosaur, named *Diplodocus carnegiei* in his honor.

Carnegie served as a trustee, or member of the board of directors, of Cornell University. Through this job, he learned that most colleges provided no pensions, or retirement income, for professors. "Of all professions, that of teaching is probably the most unfairly, yes, most meanly paid, though it should rank with the highest," he wrote. He established the Carnegie Foundation for the Advancement of Teaching to provide retirement funds for teachers at universities, colleges, and technical schools. To be accepted to the program, a college had to meet certain requirements. Many colleges and universities raised their academic standards to become eligible for the funds.

The gifts that meant the most to Carnegie held sentimental ties. As a boy, he had been barred from the exclusive Pittencrieff estate in Dunfermline. In 1902 he purchased the estate and gave it to his hometown as a public park. He also created a fund to bring "sweetness and light" to the residents of Dunfermline. Money from this fund was used to build swimming pools, a gymnasium, a medical and dental clinic, a free music school for children, and a host of other programs.

As Carnegie advanced in years, his great passion became world peace. Ever since witnessing the horrors of the Civil War, he believed that "the foulest stain upon the civilization of today is that instead of settling international [disputes] as we do personal disputes by appeal to the courts, we persist in the savage practice of killing each other in battle like wild beasts." He built three magnificent world courts, called Peace Palaces, in Washington, D.C.; Cartago, Costa Rica; and the Hague in the Netherlands. He hoped that countries would settle international disputes at these courts rather than on the battlefield.

Carnegie thought peace could be obtained if everyone in the world spoke one language. He established an organization called the Simplified Spelling Board, charged with simplifying English, which he hoped would become the world's unifying language. The board established new spellings for about three hundred words: "enuf" for "enough," "tho" for "though," "thru" for "through." Famous authors pledged to use the new spellings to help promote the switch. But the press ridiculed Carnegie's scheme. After pouring money into the project for several years, he gave up on it and moved on to his next philanthropic endeavor.

In 1904 a massive explosion at a coal mine in Harwick, Pennsylvania, claimed 179 lives. Two men, Selwyn Taylor and Daniel Lyle, rushed to the scene and led a rescue party into the mine to look for survivors. They both lost their lives trying to save others. Moved by the story, Carnegie created the Carnegie Hero Fund Commission to celebrate "heroes of peace."

Moved by a 1904 coal mine disaster that claimed the lives of miners and rescuers, Carnegie created his Hero Fund Commission.

The fund provided a pension for heroes (and their families) who became injured or died attempting to save others. The Hero Fund held a special place in Carnegie's heart. He expanded its scope and established similar organizations in Great Britain, France, Germany, Italy, Belgium, Norway, Sweden, the Netherlands, Switzerland, and Denmark.

Carnegie established the Carnegie Endowment for International Peace in 1910. Created on his seventy-fifth birthday, the organization sought "to hasten the abolition of war, the foulest blot upon our civilization." With his characteristic optimism, Carnegie said that when world peace had been attained, the foundation could use any remaining money to wipe out other kinds of evil and advance the happiness of humankind.

It seemed everyone had a different opinion as to how Carnegie should dispose of his fortune. Many groups wanted a part of it. Religious leaders complained that he didn't give enough to churches. Private schools and orphanages also wanted their share. Every day Carnegie received between four hundred and five hundred letters asking for money. He often complained that he worked harder giving away his money than he had earning it. "The final dispensation of one's wealth preparing for the final exit is I found a heavy task. . . . You have no idea the strain I have been under," he wrote to a friend. No matter how fast he gave his money away, he just couldn't seem to get rid of it all. Interest payments, earned on his share of the sale of Carnegie Steel, kept adding to his fortune. He feared he would die in disgrace after all.

In 1911 Carnegie created the Carnegie Corporation of New York, the largest philanthropic fund of its time. He transferred $125 million to the corporation, whose goal was to promote "the advancement and diffusion of knowledge and understanding among the people of the United States." The corporation gave money to nonprofit groups for educational projects that promised to have a positive impact on society. With the creation of the corporation, Carnegie had given away 90 percent of his wealth.

At age seventy-six, Carnegie felt healthy and full of life. He attributed his vigor to the "heaven on earth" he had found at Skibo, his Scottish castle. A constant stream of guests filled the castle—authors, political leaders, philosophers—people who stimulated Carnegie's mind. His guests included the writers Mark Twain and Rudyard Kipling and African American leader Booker T. Washington. King Edward VII of England even dropped by once for a visit.

Life at Skibo was never dull. At eight o'clock every morning, a Scottish piper in traditional Highland dress awoke the guests by circling the grounds playing bagpipes. At breakfast, organ music floated over the kippers and porridge. For entertainment, guests fished in trout-filled lakes, swam in an enclosed pool filled with seawater, played golf on a nine-hole course, hunted, or took sea cruises on Carnegie's yacht. The Carnegies employed eighty-five servants to run the household.

Louise sometimes grew tired of the crowds and managing the staff, so the family spent three weeks each year at Aultnagar, a lodge high in the countryside behind Skibo. Carnegie used the time to share stories of Scottish history with Margaret, called Baba by her adoring parents. Carnegie recalled the stories Uncle Lauder had told him as a boy and taught Margaret the poetry of Robert Burns and passages from Shakespeare. Those three-week getaways became precious to all three Carnegies.

Between leisure activities, Carnegie continued to write. "No fishing yet, bad winds, but I'm golfing, yachting and writing, last the sweetest of all," he told a friend. He worked on his autobiography and wrote articles for magazines and newspapers. He wrote passionately about things close to his heart. Optimistic and upbeat, his writing always ended with the hope of a brighter future. In all, Carnegie wrote eight books and sixty-three magazine articles during his lifetime. Ten of his speeches were printed in pamphlet form. He also wrote hundreds of letters to newspapers in the United States and Great Britain.

Much of Carnegie's writing centered on preventing war. He urged countries to resolve conflicts through international negotiations. He wrote about a "League of Peace" and the world courts he had funded to settle international disputes. He wrote to presidents, kings, ambassadors, and heads of state, sometimes irritating them with his enthusiasm. He focused on former U.S. President Theodore Roosevelt and Kaiser Wilhelm II of Germany. If he could get the two leaders together to talk, he felt, they could work out a plan for world peace. Just when he thought he was making progress, in the summer of 1914, World War I broke out in Europe. Devastated, Carnegie changed overnight into a tired, sick, old man. "Optimist as he always was and tried to be, even in the failure of his hopes, the world disaster was too much. His heart was broken," wrote Louise.

Because Scotland was part of Great Britain, its assets were needed for the war effort. At Skibo the British army seized Carnegie's horses. Soldiers cut down trees on the estate, because wood was one of the army's most pressing needs. Young men on the Skibo staff left to join the military. Household servants were kept busy sewing and knitting uniforms for the troops. In September 1914, with the war raging, the Carnegies left Skibo and returned to the United States.

They purchased a summer home, a stone mansion called Shadowbrook near Lenox, Massachusetts. The beautiful wooded scenery seemed to lift Carnegie's spirits. He spent his time fishing, reading, and waiting for the war to end, which it finally did in the fall of 1918.

On April 22, 1919, his thirty-second wedding anniversary, a frail and feeble Andrew Carnegie walked his daughter Margaret down the aisle at her wedding to Roswell Miller. The ceremony took place at the Carnegie home in New York. In May Louise and Andrew returned to Shadowbrook, where eighty-three-year-old Andrew died in his sleep on August 11.

Margaret Carnegie Miller and her husband, officer Roswell Miller. The couple married on April 22, 1919.

Louise Carnegie mourns the death of her husband, Andrew.

Thousands mourned Carnegie's death. Louise received hundreds of letters and telegrams of condolence from around the world. U.S. secretary of state Elihu Root called Carnegie "the kindliest man I ever knew. Wealth had brought to him no hardening of the heart, nor made him forget the dreams of his youth."

Newspapers all over the world printed profiles of Carnegie's life and speculated about how much money he had left. People were stunned when his will revealed that he had given away more than $350 million. Of the $30 million remaining, Carnegie had earmarked $20 million for the Carnegie Corporation of New York. The remaining $10 million went to private pensions for friends, relatives, former employees, and acquaintances, including former president William Howard Taft and Theodore Roosevelt's widow. The will also specified gifts for various colleges and relief for needy New York authors.

A prolific writer, a popular speaker, and an ardent pacifist, Andrew Carnegie sought to do real and permanent good in the world. In a letter to the Carnegie Corporation of New York, he wrote, "My chief happiness as I write these lines lies in the thot [thought] that, even after I pass away, the welth [wealth] that came to me to administer as a sacred trust for the good of my fellow men is to continue to benefit humanity for generations untold."

And benefit humanity it does. Eleven Carnegie institutions and trusts continue to carry out his vision for the advancement of science, education, and peace. The American Hero Fund Commission still awards medals to heroes five times a year. Thirty-five million people pass through Carnegie libraries each day, and millions of children learn their ABC's watching *Sesame Street,* a television program funded by the Carnegie Corporation. Andrew Carnegie would be pleased.

Sometimes contradictory and often controversial, Andrew Carnegie amassed great wealth while contributing to the building of a nation. His charitable gifts continue to benefit the United States and the world.

TIMELINE

1835 Andrew Carnegie is born on November 25 in Dunfermline, Scotland.

1843 Andrew enters the Rolland Street School. His brother, Tom, is born.

1848 The Carnegie family emigrates to America and settles in Allegheny near Pittsburgh. Andrew begins work in a cotton mill.

1849 Andrew begins work as a telegraph messenger boy.

1853 Carnegie becomes Thomas Scott's personal assistant at the Pennsylvania Railroad Company.

1855 Andrew's father, William Carnegie, dies.

1858 Carnegie invests in the Woodruff Sleeping Car Company.

1859 Carnegie becomes superintendent of the Western Division of the Pennsylvania Railroad.

1861 The Civil War begins. Carnegie moves to Washington, D.C., to repair railway and telegraph lines for the Union army. Carnegie becomes a partner in the Columbia Oil Company.

1865 The Civil War ends. Carnegie resigns from Pennsylvania Railroad. He forms the Keystone Bridge Company and the Union Iron Mills.

1867 Carnegie moves from Pittsburgh to New York City.

1869 Carnegie and George Pullman form the Pullman Palace Car Company.

1871 Construction begins on Lucy Furnaces.

1873 Construction begins on the Edgar Thomson Steel Works. Carnegie donates a swimming pool to Dunfermline and an organ to a church in Allegheny.

1874 The Keystone Bridge Company finishes a bridge over the Mississippi River at St. Louis, Missouri.

1878 Carnegie takes a trip around the world.

1881 Carnegie merges all his companies into Carnegie Brothers & Company. He takes a touring trip in England and Scotland and donates a library to Dunfermline.

1882 Carnegie becomes a partner in the Henry Clay Frick Coke Company.

1883 Carnegie purchases the Homestead Steel Works. He organizes Carnegie, Phipps and Company.

1884 Carnegie organizes a newspaper syndicate in Great Britain.

1886 Margaret Carnegie and Tom Carnegie die. Andrew publishes *Triumphant Democracy.*

1887 Carnegie marries Louise Whitfield on April 22.

1889 Henry Clay Frick becomes chief operating officer of Carnegie Brothers. Carnegie publishes "The Gospel of Wealth."

1890 Carnegie purchases Duquesne Steel Works. Construction begins on Carnegie Hall.

1892 Carnegie merges all his companies into Carnegie Steel. Workers strike at Homestead.

1897 Louise Carnegie gives birth to a daughter, Margaret. The Carnegies buy Skibo Castle in Scotland.

1900 Carnegie founds a trade school, now Carnegie Mellon University.

1901 Carnegie sells Carnegie Steel Company. He creates the Carnegie Trust for the Universities of Scotland.

1902 Carnegie founds the Carnegie Institute of Washington. He purchases Pittencrieff estate as a public park for Dunfermline.

1903 Construction begins on the Hague Peace Palace.

1904 Carnegie establishes the first Hero Fund.

1905 Carnegie establishes the Carnegie Foundation for the Advancement of Teaching.

1910 Carnegie establishes the Carnegie Endowment for International Peace.

1911 Carnegie establishes the Carnegie Corporation of New York.

1919 Carnegie dies on August 11 at Shadowbrook, his summer home.

GLOSSARY

apprentice: a person who learns a skill or trade from a more experienced worker

capital: money that is used or is available for use in a business

depression: a period of economic distress, marked by business failures and high unemployment

dividend: a share of a business's profits that is paid to an investor

emigrate: to leave one's homeland to live in a new country. People who emigrate are called emigrants.

endowment: a gift of money made to provide support in the future

entrepreneur: a person who organizes and runs new businesses

foundation: an organization funded by an endowment, or large gift of money

Great Britain: the United Kingdom of England, Scotland, and Wales

immigrate: to arrive to live in a new country. People who immigrate are called immigrants.

industrialist: a person who owns or manages a large manufacturing facility

invest: to give money to a business in order to earn a share of the business' profits

labor union: an organization of employees formed to bargain with an employer

majority interest: the largest share of investment in a business

monarchy: a state or government ruled by nobility

nobility: a small group of individuals who inherit political power in a nation

partnership: a company formed by two or more people, who agree to share ownership and control of the business

pension: money paid to someone to support him or her during retirement

philanthropy: charitable giving intended to help humankind

republic: a government run by elected officials

share: a portion of ownership in a company

stock: the right of ownership in a company. Stock is divided into shares.

strike: to refuse to work in order to force an employer to meet certain demands

telegraph: a communications device that allows coded messages to be sent over electric wires

trust: money or property held by one person or group for the benefit of others

MAJOR CARNEGIE INSTITUTIONS

Carnegie Corporation of New York, New York City
<http://www.carnegie.org>
The corporation was created to promote peace and education, largely through research.

Carnegie Council on Ethics and International Affairs, New York City
<http://www.cceia.org>
The council was created to promote peace by applying ethics to key international problems.

Carnegie Endowment for International Peace, Washington, D.C.
<http://www.ceip.org>
Created to hasten the abolition of war, the endowment conducts research, holds conferences, and publishes information on foreign policy and international relations.

Carnegie Foundation for the Advancement of Teaching, Menlo Park, California
<http://www.carnegiefoundation.org>
The foundation was established to provide pensions to college and university teachers. Since 1931, it has concentrated on research to improve education.

Carnegie Hall, New York City
<http://www.carnegiehall.org>
This Carnegie-funded structure is a world-famous music hall.

Carnegie Hero Fund Commission, Pittsburgh, Pennsylvania
<http://www.carnegiehero.org>
The commission honors civilians who risk their lives attempting to save the lives of others.

Carnegie Institution of Washington, Washington, D.C.
<http://www.ciw.edu>
The institution was established to further scientific research.

Carnegie Library of Pittsburgh, Pittsburgh, Pennsylvania
<http://www.carnegielibrary.org>
Originally funded in the 1890s, the system includes a main library, eighteen branch libraries, a library for the blind and physically handicapped, three bookmobiles, and five reading centers.

Carnegie Mellon University, Pittsburgh, Pennsylvania
<http://www.cmu.edu>
The acclaimed university includes colleges of engineering, fine arts, science, industrial administration, humanities, and social science.

Carnegie Museums of Pittsburgh, Pennsylvania
   <http://www.carnegiemuseums.org>
   These four museums—the Carnegie Museum of Art, the Carnegie
   Museum of Natural History, the Carnegie Science Center, and the
   Andy Warhol Museum—operate under one organizational umbrella.
Cooper-Hewitt, National Design Museum, New York City
   <http://www.si.edu/ndm>
   Carnegie's former home at Ninety-first Street and Fifth Avenue, the
   building is a design museum run by the Smithsonian Institution.
Hague Peace Palace, the Hague, the Netherlands
   <http://www.vredespaleis.nl>
   A center for resolving international disputes, the palace contains one of
   the most famous international law libraries in the world.

SOURCES

p. 7 Joseph Frazier Wall, *Andrew Carnegie* (Pittsburgh: University of Pittsburgh Press, 1989), 402.

p. 8 Andrew Carnegie, *An American Four-in-Hand in Britain* (1883; reprint, Garden City, NY: Doubleday, Doran and Company, Inc, 1933), 276.

p. 8 Andrew Carnegie, *Miscellaneous Writings of Andrew Carnegie: Volume II*, ed. Burton J. Hendrick (Garden City, NY: Doubleday, Doran & Company, 1933), 296.

p. 9 Carnegie, *An American Four-in-Hand in Britain,* 149.

p. 11 Andrew Carnegie, *The Autobiography of Andrew Carnegie,* (1920; reprint, Boston: Northeastern University Press, 1986), 32.

p. 12 Ibid., 17.

p. 13 Ibid., 7.

p. 15 Ibid, 12.

p. 15 Burton J. Hendrick, *The Life of Andrew Carnegie: Volume I* (Garden City, NY: Doubleday, Doran & Company, 1932), 38.

p. 17 Carnegie, *The Autobiography of Andrew Carnegie,* 27.

p. 20 Andrew Carnegie, *The Gospel of Wealth and Other Timely Essays* (1896; reprint, Cambridge, MA: The Belknap Press of Harvard University Press, 1962), 4.

p. 21 Ibid., 5.

p. 22 Carnegie, *The Autobiography of Andrew Carnegie,* 37–38.

p. 25 Ibid., 61.

p. 31 Ibid., 69.

p. 31 Ibid., 43.

p. 32 Andrew Carnegie to Dod Lauder, 18 August 1853, Andrew Carnegie Papers, Volume 1, Library of Congress.

p. 33 Carnegie, *The Autobiography of Andrew Carnegie,* 76.

p. 35 Hendrick, *The Life of Andrew Carnegie: Volume I,* 96.

p. 38 Carnegie, *The Autobiography of Andrew Carnegie,* 89.

p. 38 Hendrick, *The Life of Andrew Carnegie: Volume I,* 97.

p. 40 Andrew Carnegie, *The Andrew Carnegie Reader,* ed. Joseph Frazier Wall (Pittsburgh: University of Pittsburgh Press, 1992), 26–27.

p. 43 Andrew Carnegie, *Triumphant Democracy: Fifty Years' March of the Republic* (1886; reprint, New York: Johnson Reprint Corporation, 1971), 28.

p. 47 Hendrick, *The Life of Andrew Carnegie: Volume I,* 120.

p. 51 T. B. A. David to Andrew Carnegie, 20 May 1903, Andrew Carnegie Papers, Volume 96, Library of Congress.

p. 51 Andrew Carnegie to Dod Lauder, 21 June 1863, Andrew Carnegie Papers, Volume 3, Library of Congress.

p. 54 Travel letters of John Franks, Dresden, Saxony, 19 November 1865, Andrew Carnegie Papers, Volume 3, Library of Congress.

p. 54 Travel Letters of John Franks, Vienna, 26 November 1865, Andrew Carnegie Papers, Volume 3, Library of Congress.

p. 55 Carnegie, *The Autobiography of Andrew Carnegie,* 154.

p. 57 Memorandum by Andrew Carnegie, New York, December 1868, Personal Miscellaneous Papers, New York Public Library.

p. 58 Carnegie, *The Autobiography of Andrew Carnegie,* 119.

p. 61 Ibid., 170.

p. 66 Andrew Carnegie to William P. Shinn, 10 April 1876, Andrew Carnegie Papers, Volume 4, Library of Congress.

p. 66 Harold C. Livesay, *Andrew Carnegie and the Rise of Big Business* (New York: Addison-Wesley Educational Publishers 2000), 113.

p. 67 Andrew Carnegie to William Abbott, 7 September 1889, Andrew Carnegie Papers, Volume 10, Library of Congress.

p. 68 Hamlin Garland, "Homestead and Its Perilous Trades: Impressions of a Visit," *McClure's Magazine,* June 1894. Reprinted by Patrick J. Hall, the Ohio State University Department of History, at <http://www.history.ohio-state.edu/projects/steel/june1894-garland_homestead.html> (July 30, 2001).

p. 69 Ibid.

p. 69 Andrew Carnegie, *Round the World* (1884; reprint, Garden City, NY: Doubleday, Doran and Company, 1933), 178.

p. 70 Carnegie, *An American Four-in-Hand in Britain,* 240.

p. 74 Ibid., 27.

p. 75 Carnegie, *Round the World,* 101.

p. 77 Andrew Carnegie to "My dear Friend," 18 October 1884, Andrew Carnegie Papers, Volume 8, Library of Congress.

p. 77 Carnegie, *Triumphant Democracy,* 1.

p. 77 Ibid., 32.

p. 82 Carnegie, *The Gospel of Wealth,* 20.

p. 83 Ibid., 21.

p. 83 Ibid., 25.

p. 84 Ibid., 29.

p. 85 Carnegie, *The Andrew Carnegie Reader,* 96.

p. 88 "Blood Flows: Labor and Capital in Deadly Conflict at Carnegie's Mills, *St. Louis Post-Dispatch,* July 6, 1892.

p. 89 Quoted in James Howard Bridge, *The Inside History of the Carnegie Steel Company* (1903; reprint, New York: Arno Press, 1972), 233–234.

p. 89 Carnegie, *The Autobiography of Andrew Carnegie,* 223.

p. 96 Carnegie, *The Gospel of Wealth,* 128.

p. 96 Andrew Carnegie to John Hay, 24 November 1898, Andrew Carnegie Papers, Volume 57, Library of Congress.

p. 99 Burton J. Hendrick, *The Life of Andrew Carnegie: Volume II* (Garden City, NY: Doubleday, Doran & Company, 1932), 139.

p. 101 Carnegie, *Round the World,* 309.

p. 101 Carnegie, *An American Four-in-Hand in Britain,* 138.

p. 104 Carnegie, *The Autobiography of Andrew Carnegie,* 257.

p. 104 Andrew Carnegie to American Conference of International Arbitration, New York, Carnegie Hall, 16 December 1905, Andrew Carnegie Papers, Box 252, Library of Congress.

p. 106 "Endowment History," *Carnegie Endowment for International Peace,* n.d. <http://www.ceip.org/files/about/about_endowment.asp> (September 26, 2001).

p. 106 Andrew Carnegie to John Ross, 11 February 1913, Andrew Carnegie Papers, Volume 213, Library of Congress.

p. 107   "Publications and Multimedia: Program Guidelines 1998–1999," *Carnegie Corporation of New York,* n.d. <http://www.carnegie. org/sub/pubs/guidelines.html> (September 24, 2001).

p. 108   Andrew Carnegie to John Morley, 21 June 1902, Andrew Carnegie Papers, Volume 89, Library of Congress.

p. 108   Louise Whitfield Carnegie, preface to *The Autobiography of Andrew Carnegie,* by Andrew Carnegie (1920; reprint, Boston: Northeastern University Press, 1986).

p. 110   Carnegie, *The Autobiography of Andrew Carnegie,* 265.

p. 111   Hendrick, *The Life of Andrew Carnegie: Volume II,* 351.

BIBLIOGRAPHY

Bates, David Homer. *Lincoln in the Telegraph Office: Recollections of the United States Military Telegraph Corps during the Civil War, 1907.* Reprint, Lincoln, NE: University of Nebraska Press, 1995.

Bridge, James Howard. *The Inside History of the Carnegie Steel Company: A Romance of Millions.* 1903. Reprint, New York: Arno Press, 1972.

Burgoyne, Arthur G. *The Homestead Strike of 1892.* Pittsburgh: University of Pittsburgh Press, 1979.

Carnegie, Andrew. *An American Four-in-Hand in Britain.* 1883. Reprint, Garden City: NY: Doubleday, Doran and Company, 1933.

———. *The Andrew Carnegie Reader.* Edited by Joseph Frazier Wall. Pittsburgh: University of Pittsburgh Press, 1992.

———. *The Autobiography of Andrew Carnegie.* 1920. Reprint, Boston: Northeastern University Press, 1986.

———. *The Empire of Business.* Garden City, NY: Doubleday, Doran & Company, 1933. Reprint, New York: Greenwood Press Publishers, 1968.

———. *The Gospel of Wealth and Other Timely Essays.* 1900. Reprint, Cambridge, MA: Belknap Press of Harvard University Press, 1962.

———. *Miscellaneous Writings of Andrew Carnegie: Volume I.* Edited by Burton J. Hendrick. Garden City, NY: Doubleday, Doran & Company, 1933.

———. *Miscellaneous Writings of Andrew Carnegie: Volume II.* Edited by Burton J. Hendrick. Garden City, NY: Doubleday, Doran & Company, 1933.

———. *Round the World.* 1884. Reprint, Garden City, NY: Doubleday, Doran and Company, 1933.

———. *Triumphant Democracy: Fifty Years' March of the Republic.* 1886. Reprint, New York: Johnson Reprint Corporation, 1971.

Chernow, Ron. *Titan: The Life of John D. Rockefeller, Sr.* New York: Random House, 1998.

Demarest, David P., Jr., ed. *The River Ran Red: Homestead 1892.* Pittsburgh: University of Pittsburgh Press, 1992.

DiBacco, Thomas. *Made in the U.S.A.: The History of American Business.* New York: Harper & Row, Publishers, 1987.

Engelhardt, Sara I., ed. *The Carnegie Trusts and Institutions.* New York: Carnegie Corporation of New York.

Frost, Bob. "Man of Steel." *Biography,* June 2001.

Garland, Hamlin. "Homestead and Its Perilous Trades: Impressions of a Visit." *McClure's Magazine,* Vol. 3, June 1894.

Gregorian, Vartan. "Report of the President." *Carnegie Corporation of New York: 2000 Annual Report.* New York: Carnegie Corporation of New York, 2000.

Hacker, Louis M. *The World of Andrew Carnegie: 1865–1901.* Philadelphia: J. B. Lippincott Company, 1968.

Harlow, Alvin F. *Andrew Carnegie.* New York: Julian Messner, 1953.

Heilbroner, Robert L. "Carnegie & Rockefeller." *A Sense of History: The Best Writing from the Pages of American Heritage.* New York: American Heritage Press, 1985.

Hendrick, Burton J. *The Life of Andrew Carnegie: Volumes I & II.* Garden City, NY: Doubleday, Doran & Company, 1932.

Josephson, Matthew. *The Robber Barons: The Great American Capitalists 1861–1901.* New York: Harcourt, Brace Jovanovich Publishers 1934.

Krause, Paul. *The Battle for Homestead 1880–1892: Politics, Culture, and Steel.* Pittsburgh: University of Pittsburgh Press, 1992.

Licht, Walter. *Industrializing America: The Nineteenth Century.* Baltimore: Johns Hopkins University Press, 1995.

Livesay, Harold C. *Andrew Carnegie and the Rise of Big Business.* 2d ed. New York: Addison Wesley Longman, 2000.

Malone, Mary. *Andrew Carnegie: Giant of Industry.* Champaign, Illinois: Garrard Publishing Company, 1969.

Preston, Richard. *American Steel: Hot Metal Men and the Resurrection of the Rust Belt.* New York: Prentice Hall Press, 1991.

Schickel, Richard. *The World of Carnegie Hall.* New York: Julian Messner, 1960.

Schickel, Richard, and Michael Walsh. *Carnegie Hall: The First One Hundred Years.* New York: Harry N. Abrams, 1987.

Shippen, Katherine. *Andrew Carnegie and the Age of Steel.* New York: Landmark Books, Random House, 1958.

Stiles, T. J., ed. *Robber Barons and Radicals.* New York: Berkley Publishing Group, 1997.

Swetnam, George. *Andrew Carnegie.* Boston: Twayne Publishers, 1980.

Von Hoffman, Nicholas. *Capitalist Fools: Tales of American Business, from Carnegie to Forbes to the Milken Gang.* New York: Doubleday, 1992.

Wall, Joseph Frazier. *Andrew Carnegie.* Pittsburgh: University of Pittsburgh Press, 1989.

———. *Skibo.* New York: Oxford University Press, 1984.

FURTHER READING, WEBSITES, AND VIDEOTAPES

Books

Arnold, James R., and Roberta Wiener. *Life Goes On: The Civil War at Home, 1861–1865.* Minneapolis: Lerner Publications Company, 2002.

Barter, James. *Building of the Transcontinental Railroad.* San Diego: Lucent Books, 2001.

Byman, Jeremy. *J. P. Morgan, Banker to a Growing Nation.* Greensboro, NC: Morgan Reynolds, 2001.

Carnegie, Andrew. *The Andrew Carnegie Reader.* Edited by Joseph Frazier Wall. Pittsburgh: University of Pittsburgh Press, 1992.

Coffey, Ellen Greenman. *John D. Rockefeller, Empire Builder.* Woodbridge, CT: Blackbirch Press, 2001.

Colman, Penny. *Strike!: The Bitter Struggle of American Workers from Colonial Times to the Present.* Brookfield, CT.: Millbrook Press, 1995.

Damon, Duane. *When This Cruel War Is Over: The Civil War Home Front.* Minneapolis: Lerner Publications Company, 1996.

Demarest, David P., Jr., ed. *The River Ran Red: Homestead 1892.* Pittsburgh: University of Pittsburgh Press, 1992.

Houghton, Gillian. *The Transcontinental Railroad: A Primary Source History of America's First Coast-to-Coast Railroad.* New York: Rosen Central Primary Source, 2003.

Jarnow, Jessie. *Oil, Steel, and Railroads: America's Big Business in the Late 1800s.* New York: Rosen Publishing Group, 2003.

Kent, Zachary. *Andrew Carnegie: Steel King and Friend to Libraries.* Springfield, NJ: Enslow Publishers, 1999.

Livesay, Harold C. *Andrew Carnegie and the Rise of Big Business.* 2nd ed. New York: Addison-Wesley-Longman, 2000.

Meltzer, Milton. *Bread and Roses: The Struggle of American Labor, 1865–1915.* New York: Facts on File, 1991.

———. *The Many Lives of Andrew Carnegie.* New York: Franklin Watts, 1997.

Miller, Howard Smith. *The Eads Bridge.* St. Louis: Missouri Historical Society Press (University of Missouri Press), 1999.

Simon, Charnan. *Andrew Carnegie: Builder of Libraries.* New York: Children's Press, 1997.

Stein, Conrad R. *The Pullman Strike and the Labor Movement in American History.* Berkeley Heights, NJ: Enslow Publishers, 2001.

Traub, Carol G. *Philanthropists and Their Legacies.* Minneapolis: Oliver Press, 1997.

Websites

Carnegie Corporation of New York. *Carnegie for Kids.* n.d.
<http://www.carnegie.org/sub/kids/>.
A wealth of easily understandable information, this Carnegie site includes a short biography, a photo gallery, and a quiz to test a user's knowledge.

Carnegie Library of Pittsburgh. "Andrew Carnegie: A Tribute." *Bridging the Urban Landscape: Andrew Carnegie,* 2003.
<http://www.clpgh.org/exhibit/carnegie.html>.
Essays written by Carnegie along with an accessible recording of his voice make this site unique. The site also includes photos, cartoons, and a summary of Carnegie's accomplishments.

Donahue, Bob. "The Mount Wilson Virtual Tour." *The Mount Wilson Observatory,* 2001.
<http://www.mtwilson.edu/Tour>.
This highly interactive site is rich with photos of the Carnegie-endowed Mount Wilson Observatory grounds. Enjoy images captured by the observatory's powerful telescopes.

Public Broadcasting Service. "The Richest Man in the World: Andrew Carnegie." *The American Experience,* 1998.
<http://pbs.org/wgbh/pages/amex/carnegie/>.
Special features on this site include virtual tours of Carnegie mansions, a look at the steel and railroad businesses, and a Carnegie screen saver in Mac and PC formats.

Videotapes

The American Experience: "The Richest Man in the World: Andrew Carnegie." 1997. Written, produced, and directed by Austin Hoyt. 120 min. PBS Video/WGBH Educational Foundation. Videocassette.

The American Experience: "Secrets of a Master Builder: The Story of James B. Eads." 2000. Written and produced by Carl Charlson. 60 min. PBS Video. Videocassette.

Andrew Carnegie and the Age of Steel. 1997. 50 min. A&E Home Video. Videocassette.

Biography®: "Andrew Carnegie: Prince of Steel." 1996. 50 min. A&E Home Video. Videocassette.

INDEX

OTHER TITLES IN THE LERNER BIOGRAPHIES SERIES

Agatha Christie
Alice Walker
Allan Pinkerton
Aung San Suu Kyi
Babe Didrikson Zaharias
Billie Jean King
The Brontë Family
Charles Darwin
Charlie Chaplin
Deng Xiaoping
Douglas MacArthur
Dwight D. Eisenhower
E. B. White
Ella Fitzgerald
Emily Dickinson
F. Scott Fitzgerald
The 14th Dalai Lama
Frances Hodgson Burnett
Frank Lloyd Wright
George Balanchine
Gloria Steinem
Indira Gandhi
J. M. Barrie
J. R. R. Tolkien

John Muir
Jonas Salk
Julia Morgan
L. Frank Baum
Laura Ingalls Wilder
Leonard Bernstein
Lewis Carroll
Margaret Bourke-White
Maria Montessori
Marie Curie
  and her Daughter Irène
Marilyn Monroe
Martin Luther King, Jr.
Mother Jones
Nellie Bly
Nikola Tesla
Rachel Carson
Ray Charles
Robert Louis Stevenson
Sir Edmund Hillary
Sylvia Earl
Theodore Herzl
Thomas Edison

ABOUT THE AUTHOR

LAURA B. EDGE received her bachelor's degree in education from the University of Texas at Austin and went on to study educational concepts and philosophies at the American Institute of Foreign Study in London, Paris, Rome, and Athens. She has worked as a middle-school teacher, computer programmer, and computer trainer. She is the author of *A Personal Tour of Hull-House, Macro Magic in WordPerfect 6.1 & 7,* and *Macro Magic in Microsoft Word 6 & 7.* Laura lives in Kingwood, Texas, with her husband and two sons.

AUTHOR ACKNOWLEDGMENTS

My special thanks to the dedicated staff of the manuscript division of the Library of Congress; John D. Stinson, manuscripts specialist for the New York Public Library; Paul M. Romer, professor of economics in the Graduate School of Business, Stanford University; and Bill Shank, Edward Jones stock specialist, for their valuable assistance with research; and Peg Goldstein and Tim Larson, for their superb editorial vision.

PHOTO ACKNOWLEDGMENTS